VOLLEYBALL
RULES IN
PICTURES

Michael Brown

A Perigee Book

Perigee Books
are published by
The Putnam Publishing Group
200 Madison Avenue
New York, NY 10016

Library of Congress Cataloging-in-Publication Data

Brown, Michael, date.
Volleyball rules in pictures / by Michael Brown.

p.   cm.
1. Volleyball—Rules.   I. Title.
GV1015.39.B76   1989   89-30311 CIP
796.32′5—dc19
ISBN 0-399-51537-2

Printed in the United States of America
1 2 3 4 5 6 7 8 9 10

Introduction

Volleyball is a wonderful game, one that can be enjoyed by people of all ages and skill levels. It can be played indoors or out, and has a concept so simple that a person who has never played the game can grasp the basics in a few moments. On the other hand, more advanced players develop complex tactics and a high level of skill. The game they play is strenuous and a real challenge.

Over the years, volleyball enthusiasts have created numerous variations on the traditional game that was first developed in 1895 in Springfield, Massachusetts, by William G. Morgan. Although it may seem hard to believe, volleyball was originally conceived with innings and outs just like baseball, and was intended to be a relaxing, non-strenuous game.

The sport has come a long way since its turn-of-the-century beginnings. In 1928 the YMCA Volleyball Rules Committee was reorganized into the United States Volleyball Association (USVBA), which is the governing body in this country. After World War II, volleyball began to take off internationally. The Fédération Internationale de Volleyball was formed, and in 1964 volleyball became an Olympic sport. Today, at least 50 million people worldwide play, and more than 175 national volleyball federations are members of the world-governing body.

A thorough understanding of the rules of volleyball makes playing or watching the game a lot more fun. Young players concentrate primarily on developing playing skills, as they should, but when the action on the court is hottest and fastest, it is the superior athlete, playing within the rules, who will triumph. At the highest levels of expertise, players should know the rules so well that they become second nature.

The rules of volleyball, like those of most sports, have two purposes: to protect the players, and to prevent tactics that would interfere with the action that makes the game fun and gives it its character.

There is no reason to lose a match or strain a friendship because of ignorance of the rules. This happens all too frequently, which is sad and ironic, since common sense, common courtesy, and a basic knowledge of the rules could prevent either of these occurrences.

If you want to enjoy volleyball to its utmost, whether you're a player or a fan, *you should become familiar with the rules*. The text and illustrations of this book are designed to give you a basic grasp of the rules and to help prevent misunderstandings on and off the court. For those who are interested in very specific points, the official rules in all their detail are reprinted in the back of the book. Together I hope that they will help spread greater knowledge and enjoyment of the game.

THE RULES

One thing that makes volleyball accessible to so many people is the fact that it requires a minimal amount of simple and inexpensive equipment. However, the rules that cover this equipment and the court are not simply an arbitrary set of measurements and requirements. They were carefully designed to foster athleticism, skill, and exciting action. Also, they try to insure the safety of the players. Because good players make a very wide range of rapid movements, not only on but around the court, all objects such as net supports, walls, nearby courts, and the free space around the court are covered in the rule book.

RULE 1: PLAYING AREA AND LINES

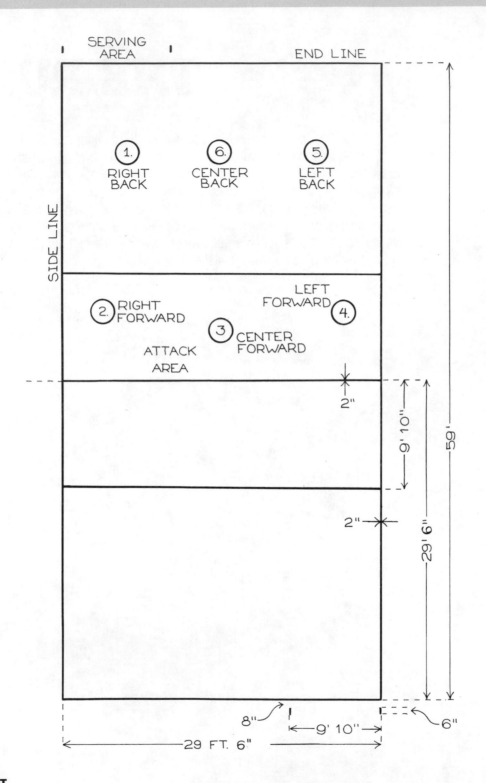

THE COURT

A volleyball court is slightly smaller than 10 yards by 20 yards. The exact dimensions are marked on the diagram. Not only the court itself, but an area a few yards around it must be clear and level. Rule 1, Article 1.

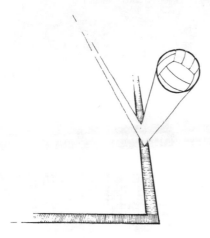

COURT MARKINGS

This ball has landed in bounds. The lines on a volleyball court are 2 inches wide. Each line is part of the area it surrounds. So, if the ball hits the line, it's in, and if the server steps on the end line, he's in too, and he's committed a fault. Rule 1, Article 2.

OVERHEAD CLEARANCE

All objects such as portable basketball goals, lighting fixtures, or tree limbs should be cleared from the space above the court. You need about 7 yards (23 feet) of clear air space above the court. Rule 1, Article 6.

RULE 2: THE NET

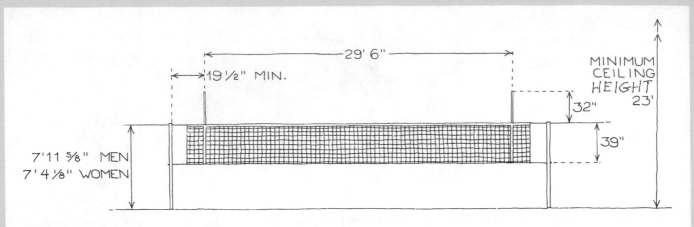

THE NET

The top of the net is more or less the height of an adult player with arms
stretched straight above the head. The net height may vary according to the
age and sex of the players. The exact measurements are marked on the
diagram. The net should be made of 4-inch dark mesh with a white canvas
border. It should be supported by cables running through the top and bottom.
If supports are wire, the wire should be covered with a soft material to
provide protection for the players. Rule 2, Article 1.

NET ADJUSTMENTS

If the net is tightened properly, the ball will not normally "die" when it hits it
but will rebound slightly. It's the first referee's job to make sure the height
and tension of the net are correct. Rule 2, Commentary 2.

SIZE AND CONSTRUCTION

A volleyball is lighter and smaller than a basketball or soccer ball. Its size and weight, and the materials and manner of it's construction, are all carefully controlled by the rules. Once you've played a few games with a good regulation ball, nothing else will do. Rule 3, Article 1

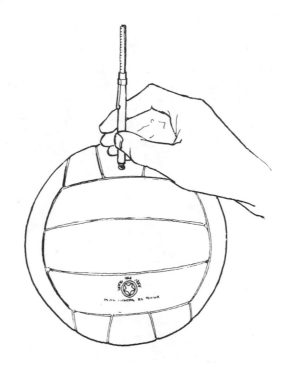

PRESSURE OF BALL

An experienced player can usually tell if a ball is properly inflated. If it seems too soft or too hard, the referee may measure the pressure with a gauge to see if it's within the limits set by the rules. The correct pressure should always be stamped on the ball. Rule 3, Commentary 3.

RULE 4: RIGHTS AND DUTIES OF PLAYERS AND TEAM PERSONNEL

Volleyball allows only very short pauses while the ball is dead; almost immediately it is retrieved, served again, and the action resumes. Time-outs are limited and brief, and a wise coach uses them carefully for strategic purposes. The ending of a volleyball game is determined not by time, as in football, but by the score, as in tennis—and, as they say in yet another sport, ''It ain't over 'til it's over.'' There's always the possibility of a comeback win.

The conduct and movement of the players during the match is carefully regulated. The rules are designed to foster a minimum of confusion and a maximum of fairness. A sense of personal integrity and honor should be enough to help a player avoid receiving an expulsion or disqualification, which can seriously mar what might have been an otherwise stellar performance.

SPOKESPERSON FOR THE TEAM

The playing captain is the spokesperson for the team and is the only player who may talk to the referees. The playing captain or the coach may ask for a time-out or substitution. Rule 4, Article 3.

TIME-OUT REQUESTS
The captain or coach may only ask for a time-out when the ball is "dead." Rule 4, Article 4.

LENGTH OF TIME-OUTS
Each team is allowed two 30-second time-outs in each game. They may be called back to back. Rule 4, Article 4, Section a.

INDIVIDUAL SANCTIONS
Shouting at an opponent who is playing the ball is unsporting and will be punished. Some other actions not permitted (whether a player is in the game or not) either during or in between games are:
—addressing officials about their decisions;
—making vulgar remarks, no matter at whom they are aimed;
—trying to influence or confuse the officials in any way;
—coaching in a disruptive way;
—trying to distract an opponent by reaching over or under the net;
—clapping hands to confuse or distract opponents. Rule 4, Article 6.

DEGREE OF INDIVIDUAL SANCTIONS
This player is sitting in the locker room waiting for the match to end. She has been disqualified, the most severe of the individual sanctions.
   There are four types of sanctions which can be called according to the seriousness of the offense:

Warning or yellow card. This is for minor unsporting offenses, such as talking to opponents or unintentionally delaying the game. The second yellow card offense will result in a red card.

A red card or penalty card. This is given for more serious offenses. The serving team will lose the service if they are given a penalty. The receiving team will lose a point.

Expulsion. This is given for extremely offensive behavior, such as obscene gestures toward an official. It means that the player is out for the rest of the game.

Disqualification. This is called when a player receives a second expulsion during the match or for physical aggression toward an official, opponent, or spectator. A player who is this badly out of control may not play in the remainder of the match. He must leave the area of the game. No other penalty is given.
Rule 4, Article 7.

RULE 5: THE TEAMS

PLAYERS' UNIFORMS

This is a typical uniform: jersey, shorts, and light, pliable shoes without heels. Headgear or jewelry is not allowed except for medical or religious medals or flat wedding bands. Anything of this sort must be taped so that it is not a safety hazard to other players. If the captain asks the first referee, before the match begins, players may be allowed to play without shoes. Rule 5, Article 1.

SPLINTS AND BRACES

Until the doctor removes this player's cast, he will have to "ride the bench." Playing with hard splints or casts on the upper part of the body is not allowed no matter how carefully they may be padded. Soft bandages and tape are allowed. Rule 5, Commentary 4d.

RECOVERY OF INJURED PLAYERS

As soon as one of the referees notices an injury, play will be stopped and a replay called. The player has 15 seconds to decide whether to keep playing or to sit down. If an injured or ill player is not ready after 15 seconds, then the team must either take a time-out or replace the injured player. Rule 5, Article 2, Section g.

RULE 6: DURATION OF MATCHES AND INTERRUPTIONS OF PLAY

NUMBER OF GAMES

Matches are won by the best two out of three games or the best three out of five games. Rule 6, Article 1.

THE TOSS

Heads! One of the team captains will call the coin toss at the beginning of the match. The winner of the toss gets to choose either the first serve or the side of the court for the first game. The loser of the toss gets the remaining choice. Rule 6, Article 2.

CHOICE OF PLAYING AREA FOR THE DECIDING GAME

Before the beginning of the deciding game of a match, the first referee makes a new coin toss. The captain who did not call the toss at the beginning of the match gets to call this one. The same two choices are offered to the winner of this toss. Rule 6, Article 3.

CHANGE OF PLAYING AREAS

After each game of a match, except when a deciding game is required, players change sides of the court and team areas at courtside. Rule 6, Article 4.

CHANGING SIDES FOR THE DECIDING GAME

Changing sides should be done with a minimum of delay. The players should take the same positions on the court they were in before the change. Rule 6, Commentary 1.

INTERRUPTIONS OF PLAY

Someone could trip on that shoe. Referees will stop the play as soon as they notice an injured player or an object on the court. The first referee calls a replay when the game is resumed. Rule 6, Article 7.

DELAYING THE GAME

This player is not allowed to hold up the match just because he's out of shape and needs a rest. Behavior which unnecessarily delays the match is not permitted. Rule 6, Article 9.

RULE 7: START OF PLAY AND THE SERVICE

It's the first service of the match. Those stomach butterflies are back again. You're serving and it would be a real shame to lose that first opportunity to score because nervousness or lack of concentration results in a service fault. The best servers crush other teams by getting into a serving groove and hitting consistently. To lose that momentum through a legal error is demoralizing and costs the team more than just the opportunity to score points.

THE SERVICE

The service is the way the ball is put into play. The player who is going to serve stands in the right rear corner just outside the court and tries to hit the ball with one opened or closed hand so that it flies over the net and lands in the other court. When the referee signals for service, the ball must be served promptly—that is, within 5 seconds of the signal to play. Rule 7, Article 1. Rule 7, Article 1, Section a.

SERVICE NOT HIT

When serving, a player must not hold the ball in one hand while hitting it with the other. The server should release the ball before striking it. If the toss is a poor one, the server should let the ball drop; if he hasn't touched the ball he'll have one more chance to make a good release. Rule 7, Article 1, Section a.

THE SERVICE AREA

So far, this service is okay. The server must stand inside the service area while hitting the serve. Her feet cannot be on the end line. In this picture, her foot is on the line marking the service area, but since all lines are part of the areas they mark, it's not a problem. Rule 7, Article 1, Section c.

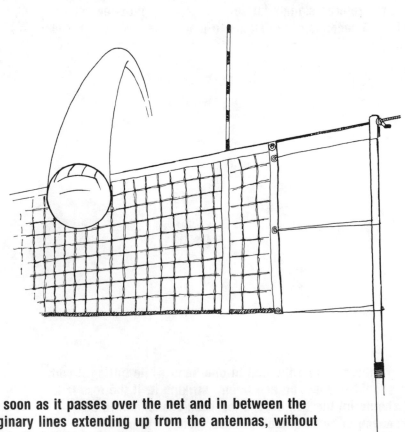

GOOD SERVICE

A service is good as soon as it passes over the net and in between the antennas or the imaginary lines extending up from the antennas, without touching anything. Rule 7, Article 1, Section d.

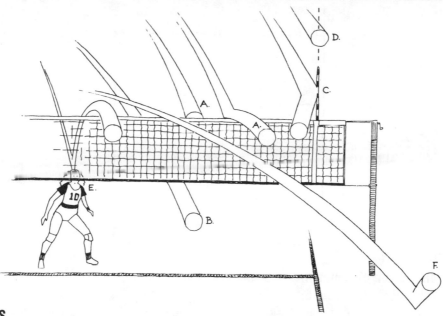

SERVING FAULTS

When there is a serving fault, the next serve will be made by the other team.
Some serving faults are:

A. The ball touches the net.
B. The ball goes under the net.
C. The ball touches the antenna.
D. The served ball doesn't stay within the imaginary lines created by the
   antennas.
E. The ball touches a player before crossing the net.
F. The ball lands outside the opponent's court. Rule 7, Article 2.

LOSS OF SERVE

This beginner is standing on the end line, and her team will lose the serve. A
player serves until a player on the serving team commits a fault. Rule 7,
Article 2.

WRONG SERVER

If a player serves out of turn, the team loses the service and any points won
during those services, and the players must move back to their correct
positions. Rule 7, Article 4.

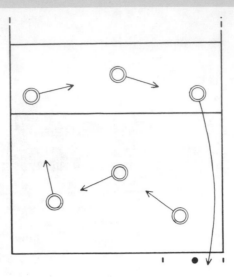

SERVICE IN THE NEXT GAME

Except in the deciding game of a match, the teams take turns having first service in a new game. Rule 7, Article 5.

CHANGE OF SERVICE

When a team is given the ball to serve, the players each rotate one position in a clockwise direction. Rule 7, Article 6.

SCREENING

The receiving team must be allowed to see. The server's teammates may not stand in front of or "screen" the server or the flight of the ball. Screening will be called if:
—two or more teammates stand in front of the server and the ball is served over them;
—a player jumps or moves in a distracting way when the ball is being served;
—the serve flies over a player whose arms are stretched sideways or upwards.
Rule 7, Article 7.

POSITIONS OF PLAYERS AT THE SERVICE

This defensive team is ready to receive the serve. All it's players, that is everyone except the server, must be standing completely on the court when the ball is served. The players should all be in their proper positions. These positions are not fixed, but are determined relative to where the other players are standing. After the ball is served, the players may move out of their starting positions. Rule 7, Article 8 and Commentary 3.

JUMP SERVE

The server may jump forward in the air over the court while hitting the serve, but he must take the jump from inside the service area. Rule 7, Commentary 1e.

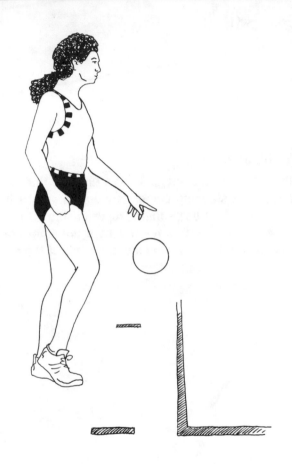

GETTING READY TO SERVE

The server is allowed to bounce the ball or toss it horizontally from hand to hand before the service, but must serve promptly. Rule 7, Current Practice 1.

RULE 8: PLAYING THE BALL

The game isn't called serve ball or rotation ball; it's called volleyball. The skill of playing the ball during the height of action is what the game is named for. It is during fast action that the experienced and cool-headed team leader makes a seemingly impossible play and inspires his teammates. It is also the time when the flustered player makes a thoughtless legal error that causes the ball to be whistled dead.

The rules in this section basically cover net play, handling the ball, and player movements. They regulate the way players may spike, set, dig and block. These rules determine the essence of the game.

MAXIMUM OF THREE CONTACTS

"Dig" and "set" and "spike." Each team is allowed three hits to get the ball back over the net. Rule 8, Article 1.

CONTACTED BALL

If a player touches the ball or is touched by it, it will count as one of the three team hits. It doesn't matter whether or not that player was trying to hit the ball. Rule 8, Article 2.

CONTACT WITH THE BODY

The ball is still in play although it hit his hand and chest at the same time. The ball can be contacted by any number of parts of the body above the waist. However, it must hit them at the same time and the ball must rebound cleanly. Rule 8, Article 4.

SUCCESSIVE CONTACTS

This block is not illegal. Any player who touches the ball more than once without another player touching it in between will have committed a double hit fault. However, players may have two contacts if they make them during blocking or while attempting to make their team's first hit on a ball and no finger action is used. Rule 8, Article 5.

HELD BALL

A player may not scoop, push, lift, or roll the ball on the body. A ball that visibly comes to rest in the hands or arms of a player, even momentarily, is a held ball. Rule 8, Article 6.

CONTACTS AT THE SAME TIME BY OPPONENTS

A battle at the net! If two opponents hit the ball at the same time and it Is held or trapped between them, a double fault and a playover will be called. If it isn't held, but squirts loose immediately, then they'll keep playing. Rule 8, Article 7.

CONTACTS AT THE SAME TIME BY TEAMMATES
Defensive confusion is costly! If two teammates hit the ball at the same time, it counts as two hits and neither one may make the next hit. Rule 8, Article 8.

ATTACKING OVER THE OPPONENT'S COURT
Nice spike! A player may not attack the ball on the other side of the net. But if she spikes the ball on her own side, her arm may then follow through across the net. Rule 8, Article 9.

ASSISTING A TEAMMATE

A player may not hold or physically assist a teammate who is making a play on the ball, but teammates not playing the ball may assist each other. Rule 8, Article 10.

BLOCKING

Blocking is a defensive tactic. When a player intercepts the ball just before, during, or just after it crosses the net, that is a block. Because of the way some of the other rules of volleyball work, it is important to remember that trying to block without actually touching the ball does not count as an actual block, and that a blocked ball is considered to have crossed the net. Rule 8, Article 11.

LEGAL BLOCKERS

Only the players positioned in the front line when the ball is served may legally block. Rule 8, Article 11, Section a.

MORE THAN ONE TOUCH DURING A BLOCK

This is a legal block. If the players blocking the ball are hit more than once, it's okay as long as the action was all part of one effort to block the ball. Rule 8, Article 11, Section b.

BLOCK AND FIRST TEAM HIT

This is extremely difficult, but legal. A player making a block may still make the first of the team's three hits on the ball. Rule 8, Article 11, Section c.

BLOCK NOT PART OF THE THREE TOUCHES

A team which blocks the ball still has three hits. The block doesn't count as the first one. Rule 8, Article 11, Section d.

BACK LINE BLOCKERS

Back line players may not block but they may play the ball near or away from the block. Rule 8, Article 11, Section e.

BLOCKED SERVE

This is illegal. You are not allowed to block or attack a served ball. Rule 8, Article 11, Section f.

REACHING OVER TO BLOCK

Blocking the ball above the net over the opponent's court is legal, but only if the attacking team has tried to hit the ball *toward* the blocker's court. Rule 8, Article 11, Section g.

BALL HITS TOP OF NET AND BLOCK

If a ball hits both the top of the net and a blocker, and then rebounds back into the spiker's court, it counts as a block. That means the spiker's team gets three more hits. Rule 8, Article 12.

BACK LINE ATTACKERS

A back line player, if she is over the attack line, may not hit the ball until at least part of it is below the top of the net on her side. The "spike," pictured here from above the net by a back line player, is alright even if she lands in the attack zone, since she jumped from behind the attack line. Rule 8, Article 13.

HELD BALL ON SERVICE RECEIVE

Receiving a served ball with open hands over the head is not necessarily a fault, although many people think it is. This type of play should be judged the same as any other openhanded pass. With fast serves it's extremely difficult to do, but on a high, soft serve, it usually can be done legally. Rule 8, Commentary 2.

BLOCKERS ANTICIPATING "SPIKE"

Players can take a blocking position with hands or arms over the net before the ball is hit. However, they may not actually touch or block the ball until the attack hit is made. Rule 8, Commentary 10.

AGGRESSIVE SET BLOCKED

If a setter has the ball blocked back into her, the setter has made a block and the team still has three hits. If the ball is blocked back into an attacker's court, that is considered the first team hit and only two more remain. Rule 8, Commentary 10f and 10g.

ILLEGAL BACK LINE BLOCKER

Back line player number 3 is very lucky that she and her teammate missed the ball. Back line players can't take part in a block. If the ball had touched her or any of the other players in the block, it would have been a fault. Since the blockers missed the ball completely, it's not a fault. She would have been smarter to wait in a ready position below the level of the net. Then, when the ball dropped below the level of the net, she could have played it as near the block as she liked. Rule 8, Commentary 11, d, e and f.

REBOUNDING BALL

A ball, other than a served ball, hitting the net between the antennas, may be played again. Rule 9, Article 1.

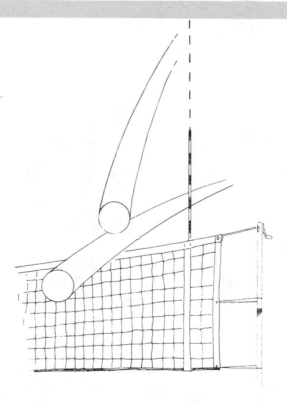

GOOD BALL

To be good the ball must cross the net entirely between the antennas or their imaginary upward extensions. Rule 9, Article 2.

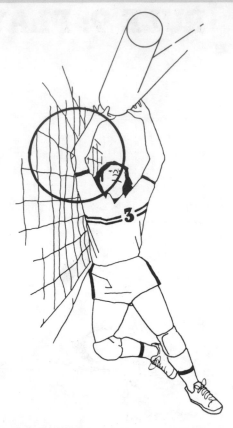

PLAYER CONTACT WITH NET

If a player touches the net, even if it's just with the player's uniform or not done on purpose, it's still a fault. If the ball is hit so hard that it drives the net against a player, that is not a fault. Rule 9, Article 3.

OPPONENTS TOUCHING THE NET AT THE SAME TIME

If opponents touch the net at the same time, it's a double fault and will be played over. Rule 9, Article 4.

TOUCHING SUPPORTS

Accidentally touching the net supports, posts, referee's stand or anything of that sort is not a fault if it doesn't affect the play. Touching or grabbing them on purpose is a fault. Rule 9, Article 5.

STEPPING ON OPPONENT'S COURT

This player is concentrating; he doesn't know his foot is on his opponent's side of the court, but it's okay. If the player crosses the line with a foot, no fault will be called as long as some part of the foot remains on or above the center line. Touching the opponent's area with any part of the body except the foot is a fault. Rule 9, Article 6.

LIVE BALL IN PLAYABLE AREA AROUND COURT

Number 15 is committing a fault, number 4 is not. It isn't a fault to cross the imaginary extension of the center line outside the court, and while a player is out there, he may play a ball that has not passed all the way over the plane of the net. His opponents' may not interfere. Rule 9, Article 6, Section b.

BALL CROSSING PLANE OF THE NET

A ball that has begun to cross the plane of the net, above the net is a 50/50 ball. It may be played by either team. If the ball begins to cross the plane of the net outside the net, the attacking team may try to return it to its own side, hoping to play it over on its third hit. The team may only do this if the ball has not yet passed all the way through the plane of the net. Rule 9, Article 7.

PLAYABLE BALL UNDER NET

If the ball is passing under the net, the attacking team may try to play the ball back into its area, as long as the ball has not passed all the way through the vertical plane. It is a fault if the opponents interfere with the player or the ball. However, if the ball, passing under the net, hits an opponent by accident, no fault will be called. The ball is dead. Rule 9, Commentary 1.

CONTACT WITH OPPONENT UNDER NET

It is unlikely that a call will be made. If a player lands on the foot of an opponent, it will be ignored unless the first referee thinks it was done intentionally to interfere with that player. Rule 9, Commentary 2.

CONTACT WITH OPPONENT BEYOND THE PLANE OF THE NET
This player's follow-through has caused him to touch his opponent's arm, but the contact will be ignored since it was accidental. If it had been done intentionally it would have been penalized. Rule 9, Commentary 3.

BALL BECOMES LIVE

The ball becomes live the instant it is legally hit for a service. Rule 10, Article 1.

BALL BECOMES DEAD

Many things might happen to cause a live ball to become dead. It could:
—hit the antenna or the net outside the antenna;
—not cross completely between the antennas;
—hit the floor or ground, things lying there, or hit the wall;
—hit the ceiling or light fixtures, or an object in an unplayable area; or
—a second referee could blow a whistle (even if by accident).
And last, but certainly not least:
—a player could commit a fault. Rule 10, Article 2.

RULE 11: PLAYER AND TEAM FAULTS

PENALTY FOR COMMITTING FAULTS

If the serving team or a player on the serving team commits a fault, a side-out will be called, and its opponents will get the serve. If the receiving team or a player on the receiving team commits a fault, such as missing the ball, the serving team gets a point. Rule 11, Article 3.

PLAYER AND TEAM FAULTS

Here is a summary of the player and team faults. It is a fault if:

—a player attacks a ball while it is completely above his opponents' playing area;

—the ball touches the floor;

—the ball is held, thrown, or pushed;

—a team has hit the ball more than three times in a row;

—a ball touches a player below the waist;

—a player touches the ball twice in a row, except when one touch is a block;

—a team is out of position at service;

—a player touches a net during play;

—a player completely crosses the center line and contacts the opponents' playing area;

—a back line player, while in the attack area, hits the ball into the opponent's court while it is completely above the level of the top of the net;

—a ball is not entirely between the antennas as it crosses the net;

—a ball lands outside the court or hits an object outside the court;

—the ball is played by a player who is being assisted or supported by a teammate;

—a player reaches under the net and touches the ball or an opponent while the ball is being played by the other team;

—an illegal block is committed;

—a service fault or an illegal service is committed. Rule 11, Article 4.

RULE 12: SCORING

WINNING SCORE

A game is won when a team scores 15 points and has at least a two-point advantage over the opponents. If the score is tied at 14/14, the game continues until one team has a lead of two points. Rule 12, Article 2.

NOT ENOUGH PLAYERS TO START

The captain wants to start the game with only five players, but that's not allowed. If a team doesn't have six players ready to start when it's time for the match to begin, that team loses the first game by default. The referee will wait 15 minutes; if six players haven't shown up yet, the next game is defaulted also. If the match is to be won by best three out of five, another 15 minutes will be waited; after that the team without enough players loses the match. Rule 12, Commentary 1.

RULE 13: DECISIONS AND PROTESTS

The game of volleyball has a strong tradition of honesty and sporting behavior among the participants. However, no matter how well-behaved your league players are, the presence of officials is a good idea—they can actually add to the pleasure of the game by allowing the players to concentrate on skills and tactics. Good officials are able to control and direct the game and make tough, split-second decisions in an unobtrusive manner. Less competent officials often are surrounded by controversy; they tend to draw attention to themselves and away from the players.

The officials should be thoroughly familiar with the rules, and the first referee should make sure the other officials understand their duties. These officials are: the second referee, the scorer, and two or four line judges.

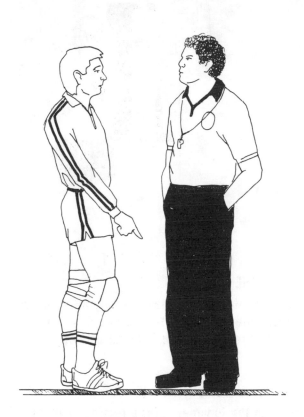

JUDGMENT CALLS

The captain is questioning the second referee about the accuracy of a call. He's wasting his breath: Decisions based on the judgment of the referee, such as whether the ball was in or out, are final and the captain may not question them. Rule 13, Article 1.

REFEREE'S INTERPRETATION OF THE RULES

Only the captain may question the referees. He may ask only about which rules are being applied and their interpretation. If there is a disagreement, the captain must mention it to the first referee before the next service. Rule 13, Article 2.

PROTESTS THAT THE REFEREE WILL NOT CONSIDER

Here are some decisions based on the judgment of the referee or other officials. They may not be protested:
—whether or not a player was out of position;
—whether the ball was held or thrown;
—whether a player's conduct should be penalized;
—the accuracy of an official's judgment. Rule 13, Commentary 1.

PROTESTS THAT WILL BE CONSIDERED

Here are some issues the captain might discuss with the first referee:
—misinterpretation of a rule;
—failure of the referee to apply the correct rule;
—failure to impose the correct penalty. Rule 13, Commentary 2.

RULE 14: THE FIRST REFEREE

The captain is concerned about the safety of the court.
From the coin toss before the game until the end of the match, the first
referee is in charge of the match. This includes time taken up by rest periods
or any interruptions of the match. The first referee is in full control and all the
decisions made by him or her are final. Rule 14, Article 1.

QUESTIONS NOT COVERED BY RULE

The first referee has the power to settle any questions that arise concerning
the match, even those not covered by the rules. Rule 14, Article 2.

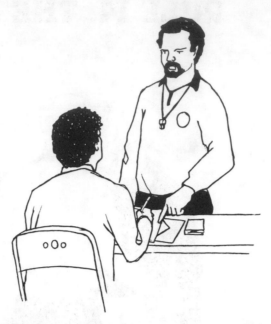

POWER TO OVERRULE

The first referee has noticed an error made by the scorekeeper. He has the power to overrule the decisions of the other officials if he thinks they have made a mistake. Rule 14, Article 3.

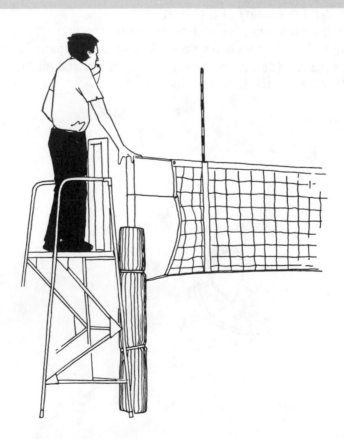

THE POSITION OF THE FIRST REFEREE

The first referee works from a position that will give a clear view of the game; the first referee stands on a platform that elevates his or her head well above the level of the net. Rule 14, Article 4.

HAND SIGNALS

After giving the signal to stop play, the first referee uses hand signals to make it clear what was called and what is to happen next. Rule 14, Article 6.

RULE 15: THE SECOND REFEREE

POSITION DURING MATCH

When working together, these two make a very effective one-two combination. The second referee takes a position on the side of the court opposite and facing the first referee. Rule 15, Article 1.

SECOND REFEREE'S DUTIES

The first referee has asked the second referee to signal whenever she sees a two-hits violation. It's part of the second referee's job to help the first referee in whatever way she is asked. Her normal duties include assisting with calls such as:

—violations of the center or attack line;

—contact with the net by a player;

—the ball brushing an antenna or the ball not crossing the net within the antennas on the second referee's side of the court;

—foreign objects on the court;

—back court blocker violations;

—any other duties as requested by the first referee. Rule 15, Article 2.

KEEPING TIME

The second referee is responsible for keeping the official time for time-outs and rest periods between the games. Rule 15, Article 3.

SUBSTITUTIONS

Substitutes should approach the second referee in the substitution zone and wait to be signaled to enter. As the substitute is entering the game and the other player is leaving it, they should touch hands in the substitution zone. Game Procedures, 5a.

OFFICIAL HAND SIGNALS

It's easy and well worth the effort for any fan or player to learn the official hand signals. One important basic to remember is that all one-handed signals are made with the hand toward the side of the team which made the error or the request.

After the signal is made, the referee points to the player who has committed the fault or to the team which has made the request.

SIDE OUT

The referee moves the arm in the direction of the team that will serve. This call is made by the first referee.

BALL IN BOUNDS OR LINE VIOLATION

The referee points to court with open hand (45°) for ball in bounds. This call is made by the first referee or the second referee.

BALL CROSSING PLANE UNDER NET

The referee points to line with open hand when player causes foot fault on service or player off the court. This call is made by the first referee or the second referee.

BALL IN

The line judge points with the flag down.

BALL OUT (PLAYER ILLEGALLY IN ADJACENT COURT)

The referee raises the forearms in a vertical position, hands open, palms facing upward. This call is made by the first referee or the second referee.

BALL OUT
The line judge raises the flag.

BALL CONTACTED BY A PLAYER AND GOING OUT OF BOUNDS

The referee brushes one hand with a horizontal motion over the fingers of the other hand that is held in a vertical position. This call is made by the first referee or the second referee.

BALL CONTACTED BY A PLAYER

The line judge raises the flag and brushes it with the open palm of the other hand.

OUTSIDE THE ANTENNA

The line judge waves the flag and points the arm to the vertical net marker or the antenna.

SERVING ERROR

The line judge waves the flag and points to the serving area.

FOUR HITS

The referee raises four fingers. This call is made by the first referee or the second referee.

CROSSING CENTER LINE

The referee passes his hand, palm up, under the net cable and points to the player who committed the foot fault. This call is made by the first or second referee.

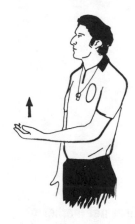

HELD BALL
THROWN BALL
LIFTED BALL
CARRIED BALL

The referee slowly lifts one hand with the palm facing upward. These calls are made by the first referee or the second referee.

DOUBLE HIT

The referee lifts two fingers in vertical position. This call is made by the first referee or the second referee.

BALL CONTACTED BELOW THE WAIST

The referee motions with hand palm up from waist downward. This call is made by the first referee.

END OF GAME OR MATCH

The referee crosses the forearms in front of the chest. This call is made by the first referee.

TIME-OUT

The referee places the palm of one hand horizontally over the other hand held in vertical position, forming the letter "T". This is followed by pointing to the team requesting the time-out. A time-out call is made by the first or second referee or by the official scorer.

SUBSTITUTION

The referee makes a circular motion of the hands around each other. This call is made by the first referee or the second referee.

BALL NOT RELEASED AT TIME OF SERVICE

The referee lifts the extended arm, the palm of the hand facing upward. This call is made by the first referee.

DELAY OF SERVICE

The referee raises five fingers in a vertical position. This call is made by the first referee.

BALL IN THE NET AT TIME OF SERVICE

The referee touches the net with the hand. This call is made by the first referee.

PLAYER TOUCHING NET

The referee touches the net with the hand and points to the player who committed the fault. This call is made by the first referee.

DOUBLE FAULT OR PLAY OVER

The referee raises the thumbs of both hands. This call is made by the first referee.

ILLEGAL BLOCK OR SCREEN

The referee, in the case of screening, keeps hands below top of head. For illegal block he raises hands above top of head. In both instances, the referee points to players committing the fault. This call is made by the first or second referee.

OUT OF POSITION

The referee makes a circular motion with the hand and indicates the player or players who have committed the fault. This call is made by the first or second referee or by the official scorer.

OVER THE NET

The referee passes the hand over the net and points to the player who committed the fault. This call is made by the first referee.

BACK LINE SPIKER (ATTACKER)

The referee makes a downward motion with the forearm and points to the player who committed the fault. This call is made by the first or second referee.

BALL TOUCHING OBJECT OVERHEAD

The referee uses an open hand to point to the player or object touched by the ball. This call is made by the first or the second referee.

WARNING

The referee shows a yellow-colored card.

PENALTY

The referee shows a red-colored card.

EXPULSION

The referee shows red and yellow colored cards together.

DISQUALIFICATION

The referee shows red and yellow colored cards apart. These calls are made by the first referee.

POINT

The referee raises the index finger and arm on the side of the team that scores the point. This call is made by the first referee.

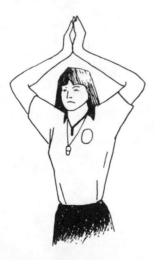

ILLEGAL CONTACT

Co-ed: no hit by a female player. Reverse co-ed: no hit by a male player. For both, the referee places palms together above the head. This call is made by the first referee.

CHAPTER 1
FACILITIES, PLAYING AREA AND EQUIPMENT

RULE 1. PLAYING AREA AND MARKINGS

Article 1. COURT—The playing court shall be 18. m long by 9 m. wide (59' × 29'6"), a clear area of 2 m. (6'6") should surround an indoor court. A clear area of 3 m. (9'10") should surround an outdoor court.

Article 2. COURT MARKINGS—The court shall be marked by lines 5 cm. (2") wide. Areas being defined by court markings shall be measured from the outside edge of the lines defining such areas.

Article 3. CENTER LINE—A line 5 cm. (2") wide shall be drawn across the court beneath the net from side line to side line dividing the court into two equal team areas.

Article 4. ATTACK LINE—In each team area a line 5 cm. (2") wide shall be drawn between the side lines parallel to the center line and 3 m. (9'10") from the middle of the center line to the rearmost edge of the attack line. The attack area, limited by the center line and the attack line, extends indefinitely beyond the side lines.

Article 5. SERVICE AREA—At a point 20 cm. (8") behind and perpendicular to each end line, two lines, each 15 cm. (6") in length and 5 cm. (2") in width, shall be drawn to mark the service area for each team. One line is an extension of the right side line and the other is drawn so that its farther edge is 3 m. (9'10") from the extension of the outside edge of the right side line. The service area shall have a minimum depth of 2 m. (6'6").

Article 6. OVERHEAD CLEARANCE—For all United States Competition, there should be an overhead clearance free from obstruction to a height of 7 m. (23') measured from the playing surface.

Article 7. SUBSTITUTION ZONE—The substitution zone is an area extending from the imaginary extension of the attack line to the imaginary extension of the center line between the court boundary and the scorer's table.

Article 8. MINIMUM TEMPERATURE—The minimum temperature shall not below 10 degrees centigrade (50 degrees fahrenheit)

COMMENTARY ON RULE 1
PLAYING FACILITIES

1) COURT CLEARANCE—In order to provide adequate room for playing of the game, a clear space of 3 m (9'10") should surround an outdoor court and a clear space of 2 m. (6'6") should surround an indoor court. If the referee's stand should present an unfair hindrance to play, a playover may be directed by the first referee.

   a. Benches, bleachers, low hanging baskets, or other objects less than 2 m. (6'6") from the court cause the ball to become dead and a replay directed if they interfere with the logical playing of the ball.

2) CEILING CLEARANCE—The ball becomes dead if it contacts the ceiling, or other objects at a height of 7 m. (23') or more above the playing area. A ball contacting the ceiling or overhead objects between 15' and 23' above playable areas shall remain in play. The ball may not legally strike above the opponent's area nor may it legally fall into the opponent's area after striking such low hanging objects. Unusually low hanging objects (less than 15 feet above the playable surface) and their supports (vertical or horizontal) shall cause the ball to become dead and a replay directed if a logical play could have been made had the object not been over the playable area.

   a. Supports for a low hanging object (such as vertical supports for a basketball backboard) are considered as part of the low hanging obstruction. Such support structures below 23' cause the ball to become dead and a replay directed if it interferes with normal playing of the ball.

   b. The ceiling and overhead objects, regardless of height, over non-playable areas are considered out of bounds and shall cause the ball to become dead. No replay is directed for such contact.

3) SERVICE AREA—Where the service area is less than 2 m. (6'6") in depth, a line must be taped or painted on the court to provide the minimum clearance during service. After service, the line is ignored.

   a) Only the server shall be in the outlined service area until after the ball is contacted for service.

4) OTHER FACTORS—The playing surface and surrounding areas shall be flat, horizontal and uniform. Play shall not be conducted on any surface that is wet, slippery or constructed of abrasive material.

   a) Indoors the playing surface may be natural ground, wood, or of a synthetic material which is smooth and free of any abrasive surface.

   b) For outdoor courts, it shall be permitted to have a slope of 5 mm. per meter to provide for proper drainage.

5) UNSUITABLE COURTS—The court, in all cases, must be under the control of the first referee before and during a match. The first referee alone is responsible for deciding whether or not the court is suitable for play. The first referee should declare the court unfit for play when:

   a) Play could be dangerous due to any hazardous condition of the court and surrounding area, to include abrasive type surfaces.

   b) Improper or defective equipment could be hazardous to players or officials.

   c) The court becomes soft or slippery.

   d) Fog or darkness makes it impossible to officiate properly.

6) BOUNDARY MARKERS—On an outdoor court, wood, metal or other non-yielding materials may not be used since the ground can erode, thus causing lines to protrude above ground level and present a hazard to players. Hollowed out lines are not recommended. The court lines should be marked before the beginning of a match.

   a) On an outdoor court, the lines must be clearly marked with whitewash, chalk, or other substance which is not injurious to the eyes or skin. No lime nor caustic material of any kind may be used. Lines must be marked in such a manner as to not make the ground uneven.

   b) Indoors the lines must be of a color contrasting to that of the floor. Light colors (white or yellow) are the most visible and are recommended.

7) ASSUMED EXTENSION OF LINES—All lines on the court are considered to have an assumed indefinite extension.

8) NON-PLAYABLE AREAS—Non-playable areas are such areas as bleachers, team benches and match administration areas (to include behind such areas), equipment storage areas near the court, and any other area deemed, in the judgement of the first referee, to be unsuitable for the normal playing of the ball or hazardous to the welfare of players and/or officials.

   a) Players may not enter non-playable areas for the purpose of playing the ball. Players making a play on the ball may enter a non-playable area after playing the ball if they have at least one foot in contact with the floor at the time contact is made with the ball.

9) WALLS—When playing the ball near a wall, players may not use the wall to gain a height advantage. If the wall is contacted by the foot of a player prior to contact of the ball, at least one foot must be on the floor at the time the ball is contacted.

10) ADJACENT COURTS—Where competition (including warmups preceding a match) is being conducted on adjacent courts, no player may penetrate into an adjacent court before, during or after playing the ball.

   a) Where adjacent courts are in use at the start of a match, the courts shall be considered in use until conclusion of the match.

   b) During tournament competition, if a court is scheduled for use, whether the court is occupied or not at the start of a match, the court shall be considered to be in use.

11) DIVIDING NETS OR OTHER PARTITIONS—Where dividing nets or other hanging partitions of a movable nature separate adjoining courts, only the player(s) actually making an attempt to play the ball may go into the net or move it. It should be ruled a dead ball and a fault if a teammate, substitute, coach or other person moves the net or partition to assist a play.

12) SPECIAL GROUND RULES—Any special ground rules for a match must be specified in the pre-match conference by the first referee.

13) LIGHTING—Lighting in a playing facility should be 500 to 1500 luxes measured at a point 1 m. above the playing surface.

14) SCOREBOARD—No special recommendations are made as to the size of the scoreboard. It should be divided into two parts with large numbers to provide a running score for each team. The name or initials of the two teams should be shown at the top of each side. Information displayed on the scoreboard is not official and may not be used as a basis of protest.

15) BAD WEATHER—In case of bad weather (thunderstorms, showers, high winds, etc.) the first referee can postpone the match or interrupt it.

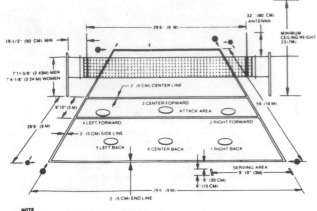

NOTE
● INDICATES POSITION OF LINESMAN WHEN FOUR ARE USED
● INDICATES POSITION OF LINESMAN WHEN TWO ARE USED

RULE 2. THE NET

Article 1. SIZE AND CONSTRUCTION—The net shall be not less than 9.50 m. (32′) in length and 1 m. (39″) in width throughout the full length when stretched. A double thickness of white canvas or vinyl 5 cm. (2″) wide shall be sewn along the the full length of the top of the net. The net must be constructed of 10 cm. (4″) square dark mesh only. A flexible cable shall be stretched through the upper and lower edges of the net. The ends of the net should be capable of receiving a wooden dowel to keep the ends of the net in straight lines when tight.

Article 2. NET HEIGHT—The height of the net measured from the center of the court shall be 2.43 m. (7′ 11 5/8″) for men and 2.24 m. (7′ 4 1/8″) for women. The two ends of the net must be at the same height from the playing surface and cannot exceed the regulation height by more than 2 cm. (3/4″).

Article 3. VERTICAL TAPE MARKERS—Two tapes of white material 5 cm. (2″) wide and 1 m. (39″) in length shall be fastened to the net, one at each end, over and perpendicular to each side line and the center line. The vertical tape side markers are considered to be a part of the net.

Article 4. NET ANTENNAS—Coinciding with the outside edge of each vertical tape marker, an antenna shall be fastened to the net at a distance of 9 m. (29′6″) from each other. The net antennas shall be 1.80 m. (6′) in length and made of safe and moderately flexible material with a uniform diameter of 10 mm. (3/8″). The upper half of each antenna shall be marked with alternating white and red or orange bands not less than 10 cm. (4″) and not more than 15 cm. (6″) in width. The antennas will be affixed to the net with fasteners that provide for quick and easy adjustment of the antenna. The fasteners shall be smooth surfaced and free of any sharp edges that might be considered hazardous to players.

Article 5. NET SUPPORTS—Where possible, the posts, uprights, or stands, including their bases, which support the net should be at least 50 cm. (19 1/2″) from the side lines and placed in such a manner as to not interfere with the officials in the performance of their duties.

COMMENTARY ON RULE 2
THE NET

1) *NET SUPPORTS—Net supports should be convenient for referees and should present the least possible hazard for players. They must be of a length that allows the net to be fixed at the correct height above the playing surface. Fixing the posts to the floor by means of wire supports should be avoided if possible. If wire supports are necessary, they should be covered with a soft material to provide protection for the players. It is recommended that strips of material be hung from the wire to alert players of their presence.*

2) *NET ADJUSTMENTS—The height and tension of the net must be measured before the start of the match and at any other time the first referee deems advisable. Height measurements should be made in the center of the court and at each end of the net perpendicular to the side boundary lines to assure that each end of the net is within the prescribed variation. The net must be tight throughout its length. After being tightened, the net should be checked to assure that a ball striking the net will rebound properly.*

3) *ANTENNAS AND VERTICAL MARKERS—Antennas and vertical tape markers on the net are required and should be checked by the first referee before a match to assure that they are properly located on the net, are properly secured and properly aligned. Special attention should be given to any exposed ends at the bottom of the antennas to assure that they are smooth and round or are covered with tape or some other type of protective covering so as not to present a safety hazard to players. Antennas are considered to be a part of the net.*

4) *NET TORN DURING PLAY—If a net becomes torn during play, other than by a served ball, play shall be stopped and a play-over directed after the net is repaired or replaced. If the net becomes torn by a served ball, a side out will be directed with the opponents serving when play resumes.*

CURRENT PRACTICES FOR RULE 2

1) NET HEIGHTS FOR AGE GROUPS/SCHOLASTIC COMPETITION—The following net heights are currently in practice for the below indicated age groups and scholastic levels of competition:

AGE GROUPS	GIRLS	BOYS/COED
17 years and under	2.24 m. (7′4 1/8″)	2.43 m. (7′11 5/8″)
15 years and under	2.24 m. (7′4 1/8″)	2.43 m. (7′11 5/8″)
13 years and under	2.24 m. (7′4 1/8″)	2.24 m. (7′4 1/8″)

SCHOLASTIC LEVELS	GIRLS	BOYS/COED
Grades 1 thru 6 (Elementary School):	1.85 m. (6′1″)	1.85 m. (6′1″)
Grades 7 and 8 (Middle School):	2.24 m. (7′4 1/8″)	2.24 m. (7′4 1/8″)
Grades 7 thru 9 (Junior High School):	2.24 m. (7′4 1/8″)	2.43 m. (7′11 5/8″)
Grades 9/10 thru 12 (Senior High School):	2.24 m. (7′4 1/8″)	2.43 m. (7′11 5/8″)

In the interest of safety for age group and scholastic competition, the height of the net shall be that specified for male competition. This height requirement shall not be modified.

2) USA YOUTH VOLLEYBALL NET HEIGHTS—Where competition is being conducted under rules for USA Youth Volleyball, the following net heights are recommended:

Ages 7 thru 9	2.3 m.	(7′6 1/2″)
Ages 10 thru 12	2.15 m.	(7′ 1″)

A higher net height has been recommended for the younger age groups in an effort to have them refrain from attempting to spike the ball and to concentrate on the basics of using three hits to return the ball to the opponents. The lower net height for the older age group will provide an opportunity for them to spike the ball as a natural progression in the overall skills of volleyball.

3) COLOR OF THE NET—Where reference is made to the requirement for the net to be constructed of dark mesh, it is currently a suggestion with a requirement for dark mesh to be instituted after a reasonable period of time to be determined by the Committee on Equipment and Supplies.

RULE 3. THE BALL

Article 1. SIZE AND CONSTRUCTION—The ball shall be spherical with a laceless leather or leatherlike cover of 12 or more pieces of uniform light color with or without a separate bladder; it shall not be less than 62 cm. nor more than 68 cm. (25″ to 27″) in circumference; and it shall weigh not less than 260 grams nor more than 280 grams (9 to 10 ozs.)

COMMENTARY ON RULE 3
THE BALL

1) *APPROVAL OF BALLS—Balls used for sanctioned USVBA competitions must be those approved by the USVBA Committee on Equipment.*

2) *RESPONSIBILITY FOR EXAMINING BALL PRIOR TO PLAY—It is the responsibility of the first referee to examine balls prior to the start of a match to determine that they are official and in proper condition. A ball that becomes wet or slippery during com-*

petition must be changed. The first referee shall be the final approving authority for all balls to be used during a match.

3) *PRESSURE OF THE BALL— The pressure of the ball, measured with a special pressure gauge, must be between 0.35 and 0.42 kg/cm² (5.0 to 6.0 lbs/sq. in.). However, the structure of the ball may affect the maximum variation of the pressure allowed; for this reason, the first refereee may reduce this margin of difference.*

4) *MARKINGS ON THE BALLS—A maximum of 25% of the total exterior surface area of the ball may be covered with logo, name, identification and other markings and coloring, which is to say that a minimum of 75% of the exterior surface of an approved ball shall be of uniform light color.*

5) *THREE BALL SYSTEM DURING A MATCH—The following procedures will be followed when using the three ball system during a match:*

   a) *Six (6) ball retrievers will be used and shall be stationed as follows: (1) One at each corner of the court about 8 m. from the end lines and 4 m. to 5 m. from the side lines; (2) One behind the scorer, if practical; (3) One behind the first referee.*

   b) *At the start of a match, a ball will be placed on the scorer's table and one given to each of the ball retrievers nearest the serving areas. These are the only ones authorized to give a ball to the server.*

   c) *When the ball is outside the playing areas, it should be recovered by one of the ball retrievers and given to the one who has already given the ball to the player who will make the next service; (2) If the ball is on the court, the player nearest the ball should immediately place it outside the court.*

   d) *At the instant the ball is ruled dead, the ball retriever nearest the service area will quickly give a ball to the player who will be executing the next service.*

   e) *During a time-out, the first referee may authorize the second referee to give the ball to the retriever nearest the area where the next service will occur.*

   f) *A ball being returned from one ball retriever to another will be rolled, not thrown, along the floor outside the court. A ball being returned should be delivered to the ball retriever who has just given a ball to the server.*

CHAPTER II
PARTICIPANTS IN COMPETITION
RULE 4. RIGHTS AND DUTIES OF PLAYERS AND TEAM PERSONNEL

Article 1. **RULES OF THE GAME**—All coaches and players are required to know the rules of the game and abide by them.

Article 2. **DISCIPLINE OF TEAM**—The coaches, managers and captains are responsible for discipline and proper conduct of their team personnel.

Article 3. **SPOKESMAN OF THE TEAM**—The playing captain is the only player who may address the first referee and shall be the spokesman of the team. The captains may also address the second referee, but only on matters concerning the second referee's duties. The designated head coach may address the referees only for the purpose of requesting a time-out or substitution.

Article 4. **TIME-OUT REQUESTS**—Requests for time-out may be made by the designated head coach and/or by the playing captain when the ball is dead.

   a) Each team is allowed two time-outs in each game. Consecutive time-outs may be requested by either team without the resumption of play between time-outs. The length of a time-out is limited to 30 seconds.

   b) If a team captain or head coach inadvertantly requests a third time-out, it shall be refused and the team warned. If, in the judgement of the first referee, a team requests a third time-out as means of attempting to gain an advantage, the offending team will be penalized (red card—point or side out).

   c) During a time-out, players may move to the sideline or to the vicinity of the team bench. All players and bench personnel may participate in discussions, provided bench personnel do not enter the court.

      1) Water and/or other liquids may only be administered in the vicinity of the team bench. Where possible, this area should be at least 2 m. (6' 6") from the court.

Article 5. **TEAM BENCHES**—Benches are to be placed on the right and left of the scorer's table. Team members shall occupy the bench located on the side of the net adjacent to their playing area. Only coaches, a trainer, managers, statisticians and reserve players can be seated on such benches. Coaches shall be seated on the end of the bench nearest the scorer's table.

Article 6. **INDIVIDUAL SANCTIONS**—The following acts of coaches, players, substitutes and other team members are subject to sanction by the first referee:

   a) Addressing of officials concerning their decisions.
   b) Making profane or vulgar remarks or acts to officials, players or spectators.
   c) Committing actions tending to influence decisions of officials.
   d) Disruptive coaching during the game by any team member from outside the court.
   e) Crossing the vertical plane of the net with any part of the body with the purpose of distracting an opponent while the ball is in play.
   f) Shouting, yelling or stamping feet in such a manner as to distract an opponent who is playing, or attempting to play, a ball.
   g) It is forbidden for teammates to clap hands at the instant of contact with the ball by a player, particularly during the reception of a served ball.
   h) Shouting or taking any action conducive to distracting the first referee's judgement concerning handling of the ball.

Article 7. **DEGREE OF INDIVIDUAL SANCTIONS**—Offenses committed by coaches, players and/or other team members may result in the following warning, penalty, expulsion from the game or disqualification from the match by the first referee:

   a) WARNING: For minor unsporting offenses, such as talking to opponents, spectators or officials, shouting or unintentional acts that cause a delay in the game, a warning (yellow card) is issued and is recorded on the scoresheet. A second minor offense must result in a penalty.

   b) PENALTY: For rude behavior, a second minor offense, or other serious offenses, a penalty (red card) is issued by the first referee and is recorded on the scoresheet. A penalty automatically entails the loss of service by the offending team if serving, or if not serving, the awarding of a point to the opponents. A second act warranting the issue of a penalty by the first referee results in the expulsion of a player(s) or team member)s).

   c) EXPULSION: Extremely offensive conduct (such as obscene or insulting words or gestures) towards officials, spectators or opponents, results in expulsion of a player from the game (red and yellow cards together). A second expulsion during a match must result in the disqualification of a player or team member. No further penalty is assessed.

   d) DISQUALIFICATION: A second expulsion during a match or any attempted or actual physical aggression towards an official, spectator or opponent results in the disqualification of a player or team member for the remainder of a match (red and yellow cards apart). Disqualified persons must leave the area (including spectator area) of the match. No further penalty is assessed.

Article 8. **MISCONDUCT BETWEEN GAMES**—Any sanctions for misconduct between games will be administered in the game following such misconduct.

Article 9. **TEAM SANCTIONS**—Penalties assessed against a team are indicated by the first referee showing the appropriate signal or penalty card (yellow or red) and notifying the coach or captain of the reason for the sanction. Such sanctions must be noted in the comments section of the scoresheet. Sanctions assessed teams are not accumulative during a game or match (two warnings against a team does not result in a red card, etc., regardless of the accumulative total). Team sanctions include:

   a. Illegal substitution requests (charged time-out)
   b. Delay in completing a substitution (charged time-out)
   c. A delay by a team in returning to play after a time-out or period between games (charged time-out)
   d. An illegal request for time-out by other than the captain or coach (team warning—yellow card)
   e. A third request for a time-out (team warning—yellow card)
   f. Illegal substitute or disqualified player attempting to enter the game (charged time-out)
   g. Failure to submit a lineup 2 minutes prior to the start of a match or prior to the expiration of the intermission between

games (charged time-out)

h. A charged third time-out (team penalty—red card—point or side out)

i. A fourth request for time-out (team penalty—red card—point or side out)

j. Administering water and/or other liquids at the sideline. (first time in game, team warning—yellow card; second time, team penalty—red card)

COMMENTARY ON RULE 4
RIGHTS AND DUTIES OF PLAYERS AND TEAM PERSONNEL

1) *REFEREE RESPONSIBILITY*—The first referee is responsible for the conduct of the coaches, players and other team personnel. Under no circumstances will the first referee allow incorrect or unsportsmanlike behavior or rude remarks.

   a) Only the first referee is empowered to warn, penalize, expel or disqualify a member of a team.

   b) If the captain asks in a proper manner, the first referee must give the reason for a penalty, expulsion or disqualification and must not allow any further discussion except for the captain to quickly inform the coach as to the reason for the sanction.

     (1) Should there be a disagreement pertaining to a sanction assessed by the referee, team captains may state their case in writing on the scoresheet after completion of the match.

2) *REPORTING OF RUDE REMARKS*—Other officials (second referee, scorer and line judges) must immediately report to the first referee any rude remark that is made by a player or team member about an official or opponent.

3) *RECORDING WARNINGS AND PENALTIES*—All warnings and actions penalized by loss of service, by a point for the opposite team or expulsion or disqualification of a player or team member for a game or match, must be recorded on the scoresheet.

4) *CONDUCT BETWEEN GAMES*—Any sanction assessable during play may also be assessed during the period following the prematch coin toss and during periods between games of a match. Teams shall be notified of sanctions imposed on a member(s) of their team immediately following the incident for which the sanction was imposed. Sanctions imposed on a player(s) prior to the start of a match or between games of a match shall be administered at the beginning of the next game. After lineups have been received and recorded on the official scoresheet, sanctions will be recorded by the scorer. In the case of multiple sanctions, enforcement shall be in the order in which the offenses occur. In the case of simultaneous offenses (such as sanctions assessed against opponents for offenses against each other) the sanction shall be enforced against the serving team first and then against the receiving team.

5) *CONDUCT DURING GAME*—During play, if a player stamps feet, shouts or yells at an opponent, or crosses the vertical plane of the net for the purpose of distracting an opponent, or otherwise deliberately performs acts for the purpose of distracting an opponent after the ball has been contacted for service, such player shall be guilty of unsporting conduct and a sanction (red card) shall be immediately imposed by the first referee.

6) *DISQUALIFIED PLAYER*—Disqualified players will be permitted an opportunity to remain in the vicinity of the bench for a brief period to pick up belongings, etc., provided they refrain from further misconduct. After one minute, if the player has not departed, the captain should be warned that further delay will result in a default. If the player has not departed within a 10 to 15 second interval after the warning, the game should be defaulted.

7) *DISQUALIFICATION FOR MORE THAN MATCH*—If the first referee feels that a player or team member has committed a serious unsportsmanlike act that warrants disqualification from more than the match in which the act was discovered, or for acts committed between matches, a report must be made to the authorities in charge of the tournament for final action. First referees are authorized to disqualify players for one match only.

8) *TEAM BENCHES*—Coaches, trainers and other nonplaying team members shall be seated on the team bench. Substitutes shall remain seated on the team bench or standing or warming up in the designated warmup area adjacent to the playing area occupied by their team.

   a. The warmup area shall be beyond the team bench nearest the end line of their playing area and not nearer the court than the team bench. Team members may not use a ball for warmup ac-

tivity during a match except during the period between games.

     (1) If no area is available for warmup beyond the bench area and away from the court, players must remain on the bench.

   b. Trainers or doctors may leave their seat on the bench for the purpose of administering assistance to substitutes on the bench.

   c. Team members shall occupy the bench located on the side of the net adjacent to their playing area and shall immediately change benches at the end of each game and when teams change playing areas in the middle of a deciding game of a match.

   d. A team member guilty of misconduct on the bench shall be sanctioned by the first referee. If the individual cannot be identified, the sanction shall be imposed against the head coach, or individual responsible for bench conduct if the head coach is not on the bench.

9) *PLAYING CAPTAIN*—One of the six players on the court shall be designated as the playing captain. The captain designated on the lineup sheet submitted at the start of the game shall remain the playing captain at all times when in the game. When replaced, the captain shall designate another player to assume the duties of captain until replaced or the designated captain returns to the game.

10) *HEAD COACH*—One person on the team roster must be designated as the head coach. That person may request time-outs or substitutions when not in the game as a player, or when in the game as a player if designated as the playing captain on the lineup sheet. The head coach shall be seated on the bench nearest the scorer and is responsible for actions of team members on the bench.

11) *COACHING*—Non-disruptive coaching is permitted. Acts deemed disruptive by the first referee shall be sanctioned as a major offense without warning. A second such act by a coach or other team member shall result in the head coach being expelled from the game. If the head coach is not in the bench area, the person responsible for bench conduct shall be expelled. Examples of disruptive acts are:

   a) Tactics designed to delay the game.

   b) Continual jumping up from the bench.

   c) Pacing in the bench area.

   d) Loud or abusive language.

   e) Comments to opposing teams, and/or officials.

   f) Throwing of objects.

   g) Displaying disgust in an overt manner.

12) *ELECTRONIC AIDS*—Electronic devices, such as video recorders, tape recorders, etc., may be used as aids to obtain information for use in post match analyzation. Electronic devices which transmit information from other parts of a facility to the bench area during a match are not considered to be in the spirit of volleyball and shall not be allowed. Discovery of teams using such devices in the bench area shall result in the coach being penalized (red card) for unsporting conduct, and the devices must be removed.

13) *TIME-OUT PERIODS*—If a captain or coach of either team asks the second referee for a time-out after the first referee has blown the whistle for service, the second referee must refuse the request. If, however, the second referee blows the whistle and play is stopped, the team making the request shall not be penalized, but the request will be denied and the first referee shall direct a playover.

   a) Teams granted a legal time-out may terminate the time-out period at any time they indicate that they are ready to resume play. If the opponents wish to extend the time-out period, that team shall be required to take a team time-out.

   b) if a team fails to return to play immediately upon the signal indicating the end of a time-out period, that team shall be charged a time-out. If such time-out is the first or second time-out, the team may use the 30 seconds. If the delay is after a team has used its two time-outs, the team shall be sanctioned (point or side out) and may not use the 30 seconds.

   c) If a team makes a third request for a time-out, the request shall be refused and the team warned by the first referee. If the request is inadvertently granted, the time-out shall be terminated immediately upon discovery and the team warned. Any additional requests shall result in a penalty (point or side out). If, in the first referee's opinion, a third request for time-out is made as a means of gaining an advantage, it shall be charged as a serious offense and the team penalized (point or side out).

   d) If a player or team member, other than the designated coach or playing captain, requests a time-out, the request will be denied and the team warned. If the request results in the granting of a time-out, it shall be terminated immediately upon discovery of the illegal request and the team warned.

RULE 5. THE TEAMS

Article 1. PLAYERS' UNIFORMS—The playing uniform shall consist of jersey, shorts and light and pliable shoes (rubber or leather soles without heels).

a) It is forbidden to wear head gear or jewelry (including taped earrings, string bracelets, etc.), with the exception of medical medallions, religious medallions, or flat wedding bands. If worn, medical and religious medallions must be taped under the uniform. If a ring, other than a flat wedding band, cannot be removed, it must be taped in such a manner as to not create a safety hazard for other personnel. If requested by a team captain before the match commences, the first referee may grant permission for one or more players to play without shoes.

   1) It is forbidden for Junior Olympic age players to wear jewelry.

b) Players' jerseys must be marked with numbers not less than 8 cm. (3") in height on the chest and not less than 15 cm. (6") in height on the on the back. Numbers shall be located on the jersey in such a position that they are clearly visible. Numbers shall be in a color clearly contrasting to that of the jersey. For United States competition, shirts may be numbered from 1 through 99 inclusive.

c) Members of a team must appear on the court dressed in clean presentable uniforms (jerseys and shorts, pants or culottes) of the same color, style, cut and trim. If tights, leotards, body suits, bicycle shorts, etc., are worn in such a manner that they are exposed, they will be considered to be a part of the uniform and must be worn by all team members and must be identical. For the purpose of identical uniforms, shoes and socks are not considered a part of the uniform and are not required to be identical for team members. During cold weather, it is permissible for teams to wear identical training suits provided they are numbered in accordance with the specifications of paragraph b) above and are of the same color, style, cut and trim.

Article 2. COMPOSITION OF TEAMS AND SUBSTITUTIONS—A team shall consist of six players regardless of circumstances. The composition of a complete team, including substitutes, may not exceed twelve players.

a) Before the start of each match, including during tournament play, teams shall submit a roster listing all players, including substitutes, and the uniform number each player will wear. Rosters shall also indicate the designated head coach. Once the roster has been submitted to the second referee or scorer, no changes may be made.

b) At least two minutes before the start of a match and prior to the expiration of the intermission between games, the head coach or captain shall submit to the scorer a lineup of players who will be starting the game and the position in the service order each will play. Lineups will be submitted on the official lineup sheets provided by the scorer. Players shall be listed on the lineup sheet in the floor position they shall occupy at the start of the game. After the lineup sheets have been received by the scorer, no changes may be made. Errors in lineups entered on the scoresheet may be corrected if necessitated due to a scorer error or omission. Players listed on the lineup sheets may be replaced prior to the start of play through a substitution request by the team coach or captain under the provisions of paragraph e) below. One of the players on the lineup sheet must be designated as the playing captain. Prior to the start of play, opponents will not be permitted to see the lineup submitted by the opposing team.

c) Substitutes, coaches and non-playing members of the team shall be on the side of the court opposite the first referee.

d) Substitution of players may be made on the request of either the playing captain on the court or the designated head coach off the court when the ball is dead and when recognized by either referee. A team is allowed a maximum of six (6) team substitutions in any one game. Before entering the game, a substitute must report to the second referee in proper playing uniform ready to enter upon the floor when authorization is given. If the requested substitution is not completed immediately, the team will be charged with a time-out and shall be allowed to use such time-out unless it has already used the allowable number of time-outs. In case the team has already exhausted the allowable two time-outs, the team shall be penalized by point or side out and may not use the time.

e) The captain or coach requesting a substitution(s) shall indicate the number of substitutions desired and shall report to the second referee the numbers of players involved in the substitution. If the coach or captain fails to indicate that more than one substitution is desired, the first or second referee shall refuse any additional substitute(s) until the next legal opportunity. Following a completed substitution, a team may not request a new substitution until play has resumed and the ball is dead again or until a time-out has been requested and granted to either team. During a legal charged time-out, any number or requests for substitution may be made by either team. Immediately following a time-out, an additional request for substitution may be made.

f) A player starting a game may be replaced only once by a substitute and may subsequently enter the game once, but in the original position in the serving order in relation to other teammates. Only the original starter may replace a substitute during the same game. There may be a maximum of two players participating in any one position in the service order (except in case of accident or injury requiring abnormal substitution under the provision of paragraph h) below). If an illegal substitution request is made (i.e., excess player entry, excess team substitution, wrong position entry, etc.) the request will be refused and the team charged a time-out. At the expiration of the time-out period, if a substitution is still desired, a new request must be made.

g) If a player becomes injured and cannot continue playing within 15 seconds, such player must be replaced. After that brief period, if the team desires to have the player remain in the game, and if the player cannot continue to play immediately, the team must use a charged time-out. If the player is replaced, regardless of time required to safely remove the player from the court, no time-out shall be charged.

h) If through accident or injury a player is unable to play and substitution cannot be made under the provision of paragraph f), or if the team has used its allowable six (6) team substitutions, such player may be replaced in the following priority without penalty:

  (1) By any substitute who has not participated in the game.

  (2) By the player who played in the position of the injured player.

  (3) By any substitute, regardless of position previously played.

Players removed from the game under the abnormal substitution provisions of paragraph h), or substitutes whose injuries create an abnormal substitution due to their inability to enter the game to replace an injured player, will not be permitted to participate in the remainder of the game.

i) If through injury or accident a player is unable to play and substitution cannot be made under the provisions of paragraphs f) and h), the referee may grant a special time-out of up to three (3) minutes. Play will be resumed as soon as the injured player is able to continue. In no case shall the special injury time-out exceed three minutes. At the end of the special time-out, a team may request a normal time-out provided they have not already used their allowable two (2) time-outs. If, after three minutes, or at the expiration of time-outs granted subsequent to the special time-out, the injured player cannot continue to play, the team loses the game by default, keeping the points acquired.

j) If a team becomes incomplete through expulsion or disqualification of a player, and substitution cannot be made under the provisions of paragraph f) above, the team loses the game by default, keeping the points acquired.

Article 3. MODIFIED SUBSTITUTION RULES—For USVBA Senior/Junior Divisions, USVBA BB Divisions or lower, NCAA Women's competition, Recreation or other levels of competition where the capability of players would require a more liberal substitution rule to permit teams to be competitive, the following modified substitution rules may be used:

a) A player shall not enter the game for a fourth time (starting shall count as an entry). A team shall be allowed a maximum of twelve (12) substitutions in any one game. Players starting a game may be replaced by a substitute and may subsequently re-enter the game twice. Each substitute may enter the game three times. Players re-entering the game must assume the original position in the serving order in relation to other teammates. No change shall be made in the order of rotation unless required due to injury requiring abnormal substitution under the provisions of paragraph b) below. Any number of players may enter the game in each position in the service order.

b) If through accident or injury a player is unable to play, and substitution cannot be made under the provisions of paragraph a), or if the team has used its allowable twelve (12) team substitutions, such player may be replaced in the following priority without penalty:

    (1) By the starter or substitute who has played in the position of the injured player, if such starter or substitute has not already been in the game the allowable three times, or by any player who has not already participated in the game.

    (2) By any player on the bench who has not been in the game three times, regardless of position previously played.

    (3) If all players have been in the game the allowable three times, by the substitute who previously played in the position of the injured player.

    (4) By any substitute, even though all substitutes have been in the game the three allowable times.

NOTE: If a substitute is injured to the extent that entry is not possible under the provisions of 2)b)(1) or (3), the substitute will not be permitted to participate for the remainder of the game.

c) If through injury or accident a player is unable to play and substitution cannot be made under the provision of paragraph a) or b), the first referee may grant a special time-out under the provisions of Rule 5, Article 2h).

d) If a team becomes incomplete through disqualification or expulsion of a player and substitution cannot be made under the provision of paragraph a) above, the team loses the game by default, keeping the points acquired.

Article 4. WRONG POSITION ENTRY OR ILLEGAL PLAYER IN GAME—If a player participates in the game and is then found to be illegally in the game or has entered in a wrong position in the service order, play must be stopped, the player(s) removed from the game and the following corrective action taken:

a) If discovered before a service by the opponents, all points scored during that term of service while any player(s) was illegally in the game or in a wrong position in the service order shall be cancelled. If the team at fault is serving at the time of discovery of the error, a side out will be declared.

b) If the team at fault is not serving at the time of discovery of the error, all points scored by the opponents will be retained. The serving team shall be awarded a point unless discovery of the error is immediately following a play in which the serving team scored a point. In such case, no additional point will be awarded. The wrong position will be corrected and play continued without further penalty.

c) If it is not possible to determine when the error first occurred, the player(s) at fault and the team in error shall resume the correct position(s). If the offending team is serving, a side out shall be declared and only the last point in that term of service removed. If the other team is serving, it shall be awarded a point unless the play immediately preceding discovery of the error in position or player illegally in the game resulted in a point.

d) If correction of the error requires a substitution due to an illegal or wrong position entry of a player(s), neither the team or player(s) will be charged with a substitution. In addition, any player or team substitutions charged at the time of the wrong entry shall be removed from the scoresheet as though they have never occurred.

COMMENTARY ON RULE 5
THE TEAMS

1) *UNIFORM—Where reference is made to identical uniforms, it is construed to mean only the jerseys and shorts. Numbers on the jerseys must be located in such a position as to be clearly visible to officials responsible for conduct of the match. Reference to home team colors may be ignored where deemed appropriate by match sanctioning authorities.*

2) *PLAYERS' NUMBERS—Each player must wear identical numbers on the front and back of the jersey while participating in the game. No player shall participate without a legal number. Players shall wear numbers corresponding with numbers submitted to the scorer on the team roster prior to the start of a match.*

3) *COLORS—When opponents have jerseys of the same color, it occasionally creates confusion as to the player who has committed a fault and the team for whom the player plays. Therefore, the home team*

should change colors if possible.

    a) Numerals must be in sharp contrast to the color of the jersey. Examples of inappropriate combinations would be yellow numerals on white jerseys, black numerals on dark navy blue jerseys, etc.

4) *JEWELRY AND OTHER ARTICLES—If play must be stopped to remove jewelry or illegal equipment, the team shall be charged a time-out. If the team has not used its allowable two time-outs, they may use the time. If they have used their allowable time-outs, they shall be sanctioned (point or side out) and may not use the time. In cases where jewelry cannot be removed, such items must be taped securely.*

    a) Earrings must be removed. Taping of earrings is not to be permitted, regardless of reason.

    b) Braided hair with beads must be secured so that it will not present a hazard to the player, teammates, or opponents.

    c) Wearing a hard cast is prohibited on any part of the body.

    d) Wearing hard splints or other type of potentially dangerous protective device on the upper part of the body, arms or hands, shall be prohibited, regardless of how padded. The wearing of a soft bandage to cover a wound or protect an injury shall be permitted.

    e) The wearing of an ''air-filled'' type cast or a protective type knee brace, provided there are no exposed metal parts, may be permitted on the lower extremities. A plastic ankle ''cast brace'' may be worn provided all plastic parts are fully covered.

    f) Prosthetic limbs may be worn provided they are of a type approved by the Regional Commissioner or Chairman of the United States Volleyball Rules Commission. The devices must be fully covered with soft and resilient padding in such a fashion that they do not present a greater danger of injury to the player and other participants than a natural limb.

    g) ''Head-gear'' is interpreted to mean no hats or bandanas. A sweat band of soft pliable materials, or bandana folded and worn as a sweat band, is permissible.

5) *LOW TEMPERATURE—If the temperature is low (about 10 deg. centigrade; 50 deg. farenheit), the first referee may allow players to wear sweatsuits provided they are all of the same style and color and are legally numbered in accordance with the provision of Rule 5, Article 1.*

6) *REQUIRED NUMBER OF PLAYERS—Under no circumstances may a team play with less than (6) players.*

7) *SUBSTITUTIONS—Only the head coach designated on the roster, or the playing captain on the court, may ask referees for permission to make a substitution.*

    a) substitutes must be already standing so that the replacement can be made immediately when authorized by the second referee.

    b) The captain or head coach must first announce the number of substitutions desired and then the uniform numbers of the players exchanging positions. Failure to indicate that multiple player substitution is desired shall limit the team to one substitute. In the event that more than one player attempts to enter, such additional player(s) will be refused entry and the team shall be warned. After making a request and indicating the number of substitutions desired, if the head coach or captain refuses to complete the substitution or reduces the number of substitutions to be made, the team shall be charged with a time-out. If the time-out is the first or second time-out, the team may use the 30 seconds. At the expiration of the time-out period, if a substitution is still desired, a new request must be made. If the time-out results in a third time-out, the request shall be denied and the team sanctioned (red card) and the team may not use the 30 seconds. A new request for substitution may not be made until the next dead ball following assessment of the penalty. (EXCEPTION: If a change in request is due to a referee's mind change, the request will be honored and no time-out shall be charged)

    c) Substitutes going on the court should raise one hand and wait by the side of the court in the designated substitution zone until permission is given by the second referee for the exchange to be made. Players leaving the court should raise one hand and touch the hand of the substitute entering the court. Such procedure allows the scorer to correctly identify the players who are exchanging positions.

    d) If a player or team member, other than the captain or designated coach, makes a request for substitution, the request shall be refused and the team warned (yellow card) by the first referee.

    e) Each time a player is replaced, except for replacement of an illegal player, it counts as an individual substitution.

    f) Each player entering the game, except during replacement of an illegal player, counts as one of six substitutions allowed to the team. A team attempting to make a seventh (excess) substitution or players attempting to enter the game an excessive time, in a wrong position, not listed on the team roster submitted prior to the start of a match, or after having been expelled, disqualified or replaced under the abnormal substitution rule for injuries shall result in the team being charged with a time-out. If the time-out is the first or second time-out, the team may use the 30 seconds. If the time-out results in a third time-out, no substitutions may be made, the team may not use the 30 seconds and the team shall be sanctioned (point or side out).

    g) When either referee notices an injured player, play shall be stopped and a replay directed. If the player indicates that play without replacement might be possible, the first referee may allow the player up to 15 seconds to make such determination. If play is not possible after that brief interruption, the player must be replaced or the team must use a charged time-out if the player is to remain in the game.

       (1) If removal of an injured player causes a delay, no time-out will be charged, regardless of length of time required to safely remove the player from the court. Safety of the player(s) is the primary consideration.

       (2) If a substitute is injured to the extent that entry is not possible under the provision of Article 2, h)(2) to replace an injured player, the substitute will not be permitted to participate in the remainder of the game.

  8) SUBMITTING LINEUPS—If a team fails to submit a lineup to the scorer at least two minutes prior to the start of a match and before expiration of the rest period between games of a match, that team shall be charged with a time-out. After an additional 30 seconds, if the lineup has not been submitted, an additional time-out will be charged. The team may use the 30 second time-out periods. If, after the expiration of the second time-out, the team has not submitted the lineup, the team will be sanctioned (red card). If the team continues to delay, the first referee shall declare the game a default.

    a) Opponents will not be permitted to see the lineup submitted to the scorer by the opposing team prior to the start of play.

    b) Replacement of a player listed on the lineup sheet shall count as both a player and team substitution. There is no requirement for the replaced player to participate in a play before being replaced. Such requests shall be governed by the provisions of Article 2e.

CHAPTER III
RULES OF PLAY

RULE 6. TEAM AREAS, DURATION OF MATCHES AND INTERRUPTIONS OF PLAY

Article 1. NUMBER OF GAMES—Matches shall consist of the best of two out of three games or the best three out of five games.

Article 2. CHOICE OF PLAYING AREA AND SERVE—One team captain will call the toss of a coin. The winner of the toss chooses: 1. first serve, or; 2. choice of side of court for the first game. The loser of the toss receives the remaining option.

Article 3. CHOICE OF PLAYING AREA FOR DECIDING GAME—Before the beginning of the deciding game of a match, the first referee makes a new toss of the coin with the options described in Article 2. The captain of the team not calling the toss of the coin for the first game shall call the toss of the coin for the deciding game.

Article 4. CHANGE OF PLAYING AREAS BETWEEN GAMES—After each game of a match, except when a deciding game is required, teams and team members will change playing area and benches.

Article 5. CHANGE OF PLAYING AREA IN DECIDING GAME OF MATCH—When teams are tied in number of games won in a match, and one of the teams reaches eight (8) points (or when four minutes have elapsed in a timed game) in a deciding game, the teams will be directed to change playing areas. After change of areas, serving will continue by the player whose turn it is to serve. In case the change is not made at the proper time, it will take place as soon as it is brought to the attention of the first referee. The score remains unchanged and is not a grounds for protest.

Article 6. TIME BETWEEN GAMES OF A MATCH—A maximum interval of two (2) minutes is allowed between games of a match. Between the fourth and fifth games of a match, the interval shall be five (5) minutes. The interval between games includes time required for change of playing areas and submitting of lineups for the next game.

Article 7. INTERRUPTIONS OF PLAY—As soon as referees notice an injured player, or a foreign object on the court that could create a hazard to a player(s), play will be stopped and the first referee will direct a play-over when play is resumed.

Article 8. INTERRUPTIONS OF THE MATCH—If any circumstances, or series of circumstances, prevent completion of a match (such as bad weather, failure of equipment, etc.), the following shall apply:

  a) If the game is resumed on the same court after one or several periods, not exceeding four hours, the results of the interrupted game will remain the same and the game resumes under the same conditions as existed before the interruption.

  b) If the match is resumed on another court or in another facility, results of the interrupted game will be cancelled. The results of any completed game of the match will be counted. The cancelled game shall be played under the same conditions as existed before the interruption.

  c) If the delay exceeds four hours, the match shall be replayed, regardless of where played.

Article 9. DELAYING THE GAME—Any act which, in the judgement of the first referee, unnecessarily delays the game may be sanctioned. (Rule 4, Article 7)

COMMENTARY ON RULE 6
TEAM AREAS, DURATION OF MATCHES
AND INTERRUPTIONS OF PLAY

1) CHANGING SIDES—Changing sides during the deciding game of a match must be done with a minimum of delay.

    a) Players must assume the same positions they were in before changing team areas.

2) DELAYING THE GAME—In order to clarify the interpretation of Rule 6, Article 9, it is necessary to explain that any attempt to delay the game shall result in a warning from the first referee. If the attempt is repeated, or it is determined that the attempt is deliberate by a player or team, the referee must sanction the player or team by denoting it a serious offense. (Rule 4, Article 7b)

CURRENT PRACTICES FOR RULE 6

1) ONE GAME PLAYOFF—A one game playoff shall be considered as a deciding game of a match and the teams shall change sides when one team has scored eight points, or 4 minutes have elapsed in timed games.

2) MATCHES WITHOUT DECIDING GAMES—In the interest of consistency, a toss of the coin should be held prior to a third or fifth game of a match in which such games will be played regardless of outcome of preceding games of the match.

  a) In the final game of a three or five game match where all games are played, regardless of outcome, teams will change playing areas when one team has scored its eighth point or 4 minutes have elapsed in timed games.

3) TIMED GAME—In circumstances where the efficient management of a tournament or series of matches requires adherence to a time schedule in order to complete the competitions, timed games may be employed. Such timed games may be played on the basis of 8 minutes ball-in-play time or 15 points, whichever occurs first. Such basis must be established before the first game where round robins, a specific number of games, etc., are indicated as the format.

RULE 7. COMMENCEMENT OF PLAY AND THE SERVICE

Article 1. THE SERVICE—The service is the act of putting the ball into play by the player in the right back position who hits the ball with one hand (open or closed) or any part of one arm in an effort to direct the ball into the opponent's area.

  a) The server shall have five seconds after the first referee's readiness to serve whistle in which to release or toss the ball for service.

  b) After being clearly released or thrown from the hand(s) of the server, the ball shall be cleanly hit for service. (EXCEPTION: If, after releasing or tossing the ball for service, the server allows the ball to fall to the floor (ground) without being hit or contacted, the service effort shall be cancelled and a re-serve directed. However, the referee will not allow the game to be delayed in this manner more than one time during any service).

c) At the instant the ball is hit for the service, the server shall not have any portion of the body in contact with the end line, the court or the floor (ground) outside the lines marking the service area. At the instant of service, the server may stand on or between the two lines, or their extensions which mark the service area.

d) The service is considered good if the ball passes over the net between the antennas or their indefinite extensions without touching the net or other objects.

e) If the ball is served before the first referee's whistle, the serve shall be cancelled and a re-serve directed. The first referee will not allow a player to delay the game in this manner more than one time.

Article 2. SERVING FAULTS—The referee will signal side-out and direct a change of service to the other team when one of the following serving faults occur:
a) The ball touches the net.
b) The ball passes under the net.
c) The ball touches an antenna or does not pass over the net completely between the antennas or their indefinite extensions.
d) The ball touches a player of the serving team or any object before entering the opponent's playing area.
e) The ball lands outside the limits of the opponent's playing area.

Article 3. DURATION OF SERVICE—A player continues to serve until a fault is committed by the serving team.

Article 4. SERVING OUT OF ORDER—If a team has served out of order, the team loses the service and any points gained during such out of order service. The players of the team at fault must immediately resume their correct positions on the court.

Article 5. SERVICE IN SUBSEQUENT GAMES—The team not serving first in the preceding game of a match shall serve first in the next game of the match, except in the deciding game of a match (Rule 6, Article 3).

Article 6. CHANGE OF SERVICE—The team which receives the ball for service shall rotate one position clockwise before serving.

Article 7. SCREENING—The players of the serving team must not, through screening, prevent the receiving player from watching the server or trajectory of the ball. Screening is illegal and a fault.
a) A team makes a group screen when the server is hidden behind a group of two or more teammates and the ball is served over a member(s) of the group.
b) A player(s) who jumps or moves in a distracting manner at the moment of service shall be guilty of screening.
c) A player with hands extended clearly above the height of the head or arms extended sideways at service shall be considered to be screening if the ball passes over the player.

Article 8. POSITIONS OF PLAYERS AT SERVICE—At the time the ball is contacted for the serve, the placement of players on the court must conform to the service order recorded on the scoresheet as follows (the server is exempt from this requirement):
a) In the front line, the center forward (3) may not be as near the right sideline as the right forward (2) nor as near the left sideline as the left forward (4). In the back line, the center back (6) may not be as near the right sideline as the right back (1) nor as near the left sideline as the left back (5). No back line player may be as near the net as the corresponding front line player. After the ball is contacted for the serve, players may move from their respective positions.
b) The serving order as recorded on the official scoresheet must remain the same until the game is completed.
c) Before the start of a new game, the serving order may be changed and such changes must be recorded on the scoresheet. It is the responsibility of the head coach or team captain to submit a lineup to the scorer prior to the expiration of the authorized rest period between games of a match.

COMMENTARY ON RULE 7
COMMENCEMENT OF PLAY AND THE SERVICE

1) *THE SERVICE—If the server releases or tosses the ball for service, but does not hit it and it touches some part of the server's body or*

uniform as it falls, this counts as an illegal service and the ball shall be given to the other team.

a) *If the server releases or tosses the ball in a service action and then allows it to fall to the floor (ground) without touching it, the first referee shall cancel the serve and direct a second and last attempt at service (re-serve) for which an additional five seconds is allowed. If the player does not serve within these time limits, a serious offense is committed which must be penalized by loss of service.*

 1) *After the referee's whistle for service, no other actions (requests for time-out, lineup check, etc.) may be considered until after the ball has been served, even if the request has been made after a server has initiated service action and legally permitted the ball to fall to the floor. A re-serve is considered to be a part of a single effort to serve and must be completed before any requests may be considered.*

b) *If a player serves the ball prior to the whistle of the first referee, the service action shall be cancelled and a re-serve directed on the first such occasion. On a second occasion the player shall be warned unless, in the first referee's judgement, such action was done for the purpose of attempting to gain an advantage. In that case, the player shall be sanctioned (red card).*

c) *The server is not allowed to delay service after the first referee's whistle, even if it appears that players on the serving team are in a wrong position or are not ready.*

d) *Service cannot be made with two hands or arms.*

e) *At the moment of service, the server's body may be in the air provided the last contact with the floor (ground) was within the legal service area.*

f) *If a service fault occurs (Rule 7, Article 2) and the opposing team commits a positional fault at the moment of a legal service (Rule 7, Article 8), the server's team scores a point.*

g) *If an illegal service occurs and the opposing team commits a positional fault at the moment of service, the ball is given to the opponents. The service is illegal when:*
 (1) The players serves while in contact with the floor (ground) outside the service area.
 (2) The ball is thrown or pushed for service.
 (3) The player serves with two hands or arms.
 (4) The service is not made following the correct rotation order.
 (5) The ball is not thrown or released before it is hit for service.
 (6) Service action is not initiated within five seconds after the first referee's readiness-to-serve whistle.

2) *SCREENING—In order for members of the serving team to be called for a group screen at the moment of service, the players must be standing near each other in an erect position and the ball must pass over the area where the players were standing at the moment of contact of the ball for service.*

a) *After the first referee's whistle, no single player of the serving team may wave arms, extend arms to the side, jump or move in a distracting manner prior to the contact of the ball for service, regardless of the path of the ball.*

b) *If a member of the serving team moves to take a position in front of an opponent after the first referee's whistle for service, the player shall be sanctioned (red card) for unsporting conduct.*

c) *If, in the opinion of the first referee, a player deliberately attempts to distract an opponent after the ball has been contacted for service, such player shall be guilty of unsporting conduct and an individual sanction (red card) shall be imposed.*

3) *POSITION OF PLAYERS—The position of players is judged according to the position of their feet in contact with the floor (ground) at the time the ball is contacted for service. A player who is not in contact with the floor (ground) will be considered to retain the status of the last point of contact with the playing surface. For the purpose of this rule, the service area is not considered to be a part of the court. All players, except the server, must be fully on the court at the time the ball is contacted for service. Players in contact with the center line are governed by the provisions of Rule 9, Article 6. At the instant the server hits the ball for service, all players on the court must be in their proper positions corresponding with the order noted on the scoresheet. A positional fault should be signalled by the referee(s) as soon as the ball has been hit by the server.*

a) *Occasionally there may be doubt as to whether a player is a front or back line player. In such cases, the referee may withhold the whistle and check the lineup sheet after play has concluded. If a check of the lineup sheet reveals that a player was out of position, the call may be made, even though late.*

4) *WRONG SERVER—When it is discovered that a wrong player is about to serve the ball, the scorer shall wait until the service has been completed and then blow the horn/whistle or stop the game in any manner possible and report the fault to one of the referees.*

Any points scored by a wrong server shall be removed, a side-out declared and players of the team at fault must immediately resume their correct positions on the court.

CURRENT PRACTICES FOR RULE 7

1) PRELIMINARY SERVICE ACTION—Preliminary actions, such as bouncing the ball on the floor or lightly tossing the ball from one hand to the other, shall be allowed, but shall be counted as part of the five seconds allowed for the server to initiate service release or toss the ball preparatory for the service.

2) SERVICE FOR ELEMENTARY GRADE PLAYERS—Where elementary grade age players are in a competition, it can be considered legal service if the ball is hit directly from the hand of the server, not necessarily dropped or tossed. Where this serve is acceptable, it should be established in advance or otherwise agreed upon mutually before competition starts and the officials notified. In such levels of team play, players should be encouraged to develop ability and skills necessary for a serve which does satisfy the requirements of the official rule.

3) REQUESTING LINEUP CHECK—Team captains may request verfication of the service order of their team if done on an infrequent basis. Requests for lineup checks for opponents will be limited to determining whether or not the players are in a correct service order. No information will be provided to disclose which opposing players are front line or back line players.

RULE 8. PLAYING THE BALL

Article 1. MAXIMUM OF THREE TEAM CONTACTS—Each team is allowed a maximum of three (3) successive contacts of the ball in order to return the ball to the opponent's area. (EXCEPTION: Rule 8, Article 11)

Article 2. CONTACTED BALL—A player who contacts the ball, or is contacted by the ball, shall be considered as having played the ball.

Article 3. CONTACT OF BALL WITH THE BODY—The ball may contact any part of the body on or above the waist.

Article 4. SIMULTANEOUS CONTACTS WITH THE BODY—The ball can contact any number of parts of the body down to, and including the waist, providing such contacts are simultaneous and that the ball rebounds immediately and cleanly after such contact.

Article 5. SUCCESSIVE CONTACTS—Players may have suc-cesive contacts of the ball during blocking (Rule 8, Article 11) and during a single attempt to make the first team hit of a ball coming from the opponents, even if the ball is blocked, provid-ed there is no finger action used during the effort and the ball is not held or thrown. Any other player contacting the ball more than once, with whatever part of the body, without any other player having touched it between these contacts, will be con-sidered as having committed a double hit fault.

Article 6. HELD BALL—When the ball visibly comes to rest momentarily in the hands or arms of a player, it is considered as having been held. The ball must be hit in such a manner that it rebounds cleanly after contact with a player. Scooping, lifting, pushing, or allowing the ball to roll on the body shall be con-sidered to be a form of holding. A ball clearly hit with one or both hands from a position below the ball is considered a good play.

Article 7. SIMULTANEOUS CONTACTS BY OPPONENTS—If the ball visibly comes to rest between two opposing players, it is a double fault and the first referee will direct a play-over.
  a) If the ball is contacted simultaneously by opponents and does not visibly come to rest, play shall continue.

  b) After simultaneous contact by opponents, the team on whose side the ball falls shall have the right to play the ball three times.
  c) If, after simultaneous contact by opponents, the ball falls out of bounds, the team on the opposite side shall be deemed as having provided the impetus necessary to cause the ball to be out of bounds.

Article 8. BALL PLAYED BY TEAMMATES—When two players of the same team contact the ball simultaneously, this is con-sidered as two team contacts and neither of the players may make the next play on the ball. (EXCEPTION: Rule 8, Article 11)

Article 9. ATTACKING OVER OPPONENT'S COURT—A player is not allowed to attack the ball on the opposite side of the net. If the ball is hit above the spiker's side of the net and then the follow-through causes the spiker's hand and arm to cross the net without contacting an opponent, such action does not constitute a fault.

Article 10. ASSISTING A TEAMMATE—No player shall assist a teammate by holding such player while the player is making a play on the ball. It shall be legal for a player to hold a team-mate not making a play on the ball in order to prevent a fault.

Article 11. BLOCKING—Blocking is the action close to the net which intercepts the ball coming from the opponent's side by making contact with the ball before it crosses the net, as it crosses the net or immediately after it has crossed the net. An attempt to block does not constitute a block unless the ball is contacted during the effort. A blocked ball is considered to have crossed the net.
  a) Blocking may be legally accomplished by only the players who are in the front line at the time of service.
  b) Multiple contacts of the ball by a player(s) participating in a block shall be legal provided it is during one attempt to in-tercept the ball.
    (1) Multiple contacts of the ball during a block shall be counted as a single contact, even though the ball may make multiple contacts with one or more players of the block.
  c) Any player participating in a block shall have the right to make the next contact, such contact counting as the first of three hits allowed the team.
  d) The team which effected a block shall have the right to three additional contacts after the block in order to return the ball to the opponent's area.
  e) Back line players may not block or participate in a block, but may play the ball in any other position near or away from the block.
  f) Blocking or attacking a served ball is prohibited.
  g) Blocking of the ball across the net above the opponent's court shall be legal provided that such block is:
    (1) After a player of the attacking team has spiked the ball, or, in the first referee's judgement, intentionally directed the ball into the opponent's court; or,
    (2) After the opponent's have completed their allowable three hits; or,
    (3) After the opponents have hit the ball in such a manner that the ball would, in the first referee's judgement, clearly cross the net if not touched by a player, provided no member of the attacking team is in a position to make a legal play on the ball; or,
    (4) If the ball is falling near the net and no member of the attacking team could reasonably make a play on the ball.

Article 12. BALL CONTACTING TOP OF NET AND BLOCK—If the ball touches the top of the net and a player(s) participating in a block and the ball returns to the attacker's side of the net, this team shall then have the right of three more contacts to return the ball to the opponent's area.

Article 13. BACK LINE ATTACKER—A back line player return-ing the ball to the opponent's side while forward of the attack line must contact the ball when at least part of the ball is below the level of the top of the net over the attacking team's area. The restriction does not apply if the back line player jumps from clearly behind the attack line and, after contacting the ball, lands on or in front of the line.
  a) It is a fault when a back line player in the attack zone or con-tacting the attack line, or its imaginary extension, hits the ball while the bottom of the ball is completely above the height of the net and causes the ball to cross directly and completely the plane of the net or intentionally directs the ball towards the opponent's area so that it is contacted by an opponent before fully passing the plane of the net. (see commentary 9)

COMMENTARY ON RULE 8
PLAYING THE BALL

1) RECEPTION OF THE BALL—Contact with the ball must be brief and instantaneous. When the ball has been hit hard, or during setting action, it sometimes stays very briefly in contact with the hands of the player handling the ball. In such cases, contact that results from playing the ball from below, or a high reception where the ball is received from high in the air, should not be penalized. The following actions of playing the ball should not be counted as faults:
   a) When the sound is different to that made by a finger tip hit, but the hit is still played simultaneously with both hands and the ball is not held.
   b) When the ball is played with two closed fists on a 2nd or 3rd hit and the contact with the ball is simultaneous.
   c) When the ball contacts the open hand and rolls off the hand backward without being held.
   d) When the ball is played correctly and the player's hands move backwards, either during or after the hit.
   e) When a poorly hit ball is caused to rotate (such as a defective spike where the ball is spun and not hit squarely or a set ball that is caused to rotate due to improper contact).

2) HELD BALL ON SERVICE RECEIVE—Receiving a served ball with an overhead pass using open hands is not necessarily a fault. Such service receives must be judged the same as any open handed pass. If the served ball is travelling in a low and relatively flat trajectory, receiving it with open hands and passing without holding the ball is extremely difficult. If the serve is high and soft, the pass can be made legally the same as any similar ball crossing the net after the service.

3) BLOCKING OR ATTACKING SERVE—No player in the attack zone may block or attack a served ball while the ball is above the height of the net. Such contact causes the ball to become dead immediately and a point awarded to the serving team.

4) SIMULTANEOUS CONTACTS—The ball may contact several parts of the body at the same time legally, provided the ball is not held.

5) SUCCESSIVE CONTACTS—A player may have successive contacts with the ball when making the first play on a ball coming from the opponents even if the ball has been blocked by a teammate, providing fingers are not used in a passing action during an attempt to play the ball. During such successive contacts, holding the ball, throwing the ball or permitting the ball to roll along any part of the body is illegal and must be called. Flight of the ball after successive contacts is ignored. Successive contacts on a first received ball must be during one continuous attempt to play the ball. Players may have successive contact when blocking (Rule 8, Article 11).

6) SIMULTANEOUS CONTACT BETWEEN OPPOSING PLAYERS—The rules are designed to insure the continuity of play. During the contact of the ball simultaneously by opposing players, the first referee must not blow the whistle unless the ball is momentarily suspended between the hands of opposing players and clearly comes to rest. In such case, the ball must be replayed without a point or change of service being awarded.

7) SIMULTANEOUS CONTACT BETWEEN TEAMMATES—When two players of a team attempt to play the ball at the same time, resultant action can cause the appearance of simultaneous contact. Referees must be positive that simultaneous contact has been seen before charging that team with two hits. If there is any doubt, only one hit should be called.

8) ATTACK HIT—A hit by a player in an intentional effort to direct the ball into the opponent's court. A third hit by a team is considered to be an attack hit, regardless of intention. A served ball is not considered to be an attack hit.

9) SPIKED BALL—A ball that is forcibly hit from above the height of the net into the opponent's court.

10) BLOCKING—Any ball directed towards the opponent's area as an attack hit, other than a served ball, can be blocked by one or a group of opposing front line players. In order for players to be considered in the act of blocking, some part of the body must be above the height of the net during the effort. Blocking action is terminated when a blocker contacts the floor and has no part of the body above the height of the net.
   a) If members of a composite block are to benefit from the rule allowing multiple contacts of the ball by blockers, they must be close to the net and close to each other at the time the ball is contacted by the block. If one member of a composite block is above the height of the net during the effort, all members are considered as having been above the height of the net. If a player is attempting to block, but is separated from the block contacted by the ball, such contact will count as the first of three contacts allowed to return the ball to the opponent's court.
   b) Players may take a blocking position with the hands and arms over the net before the opponent's attack hit providing there is no contact with the ball until after the opponents have completed an attack hit (commentary 8) which directs the ball across the net. Immediately after such hit by the attacking team, blockers may contact the ball in an effort to prevent it crossing the net.
   c) Multiple contacts of the ball may be made by any player or players taking part in a block and shall constitute one contact of the ball. After such contact, the team is allowed three additional contacts to return the ball to the opponent's area. The multiple contact is legal even if it can be seen that during the blocking action the ball has contacted in rapid succession:
      (1) The hands or arms of one player; or,
      (2) The hands or arms of two or more players; or,
      (3) The hands, arms or other parts of one or more players on or above their waists.
   d) If the ball touches the top of the net and the hands of an opposing blocker(s), the ball shall be considered to have crossed the net and been blocked. After such contact, the attacking team is allowed an additional three contacts of the ball.
   e) Blockers may reach across the plane of the net outside the antenna, but may not contact the ball over the opponent's area. If contact of the ball over the opponent's area is made while any part of the blocker or member of a composite block is outside the antenna across the plane of the net, the block is illegal.
   f) If a player near the net sets the ball from above the height of the net in such a manner that the ball is blocked back into the player, such contact is considered to be a block.
   g) If a player near the net attacks the ball in such a manner that the ball is blocked back into the attacking player, such contact is considered to be a first team hit.

11) BACK LINE PLAYERS—A back line player who is inside the attack zone, or its assumed extension, may play the ball directly into the opposite court if, at the moment of contact, the ball is not completely above the level of the top of the net. If a back line player jumps from the floor (ground) clearly behind the attack line, the ball may be spiked or intentionally directed into the opponent's area, regardless of where the player lands after hitting the ball.
   a) A ball contacted from above the height of the net (including a spiked ball) and directed towards the opponent's court by a back line player on or forward of the attack line, or its imaginary extension, does not become an illegal hit until the ball passes beyond the vertical plane of the net or is legally contacted by the opponents.
      (1) If the illegally hit ball is contacted by a back row blocker of the opponents, it is double fault and a replay shall be directed.
   b) On a 1st or 2nd team hit, if a back line player on or in front of the attack line contacts the ball from above the height of the net in an attempt to direct the ball to a teammate, the ball remains alive and in play, even if legally contacted by an opposing player before the ball passes untouched fully beyond the vertical plane of the net. If the ball passes untouched fully beyond the vertical plane of the net, it becomes a back row player fault.
   c) Simultaneous contact above the net between a back row attacker and an opposing back row blocker is a double fault.
   d) If a back line player at the net, along with blockers, lifts hands or arms towards the ball as it comes across the net and is touched by the ball, or the ball touches any of the players in that block, it is a fault; back line players not having the right to participate in a block. However, if the block containing the back line player does not touch the ball, the attempt to block is not considered to be a fault.
   e) A back line player with part of the body above the net while attempting to play the ball near the net becomes an illegal blocker if the ball is legally attacked or blocked by an opponent into the back row player (including simultaneous contact).
   f) Back line players may not participate in a block, but there is no restriction on their being next to a block for the purpose of playing the ball in other than blocking action.

RULE 9. PLAY AT THE NET

Article 1.   BALL IN NET BETWEEN ANTENNAS—A ball, other than a served ball, hitting the net between the antennas may be played again. If the ball touches the net after a team's allowable three contacts and does not cross the net, the referee should not stop the play until the ball is contacted for the fourth time or has touched the playing surface. (See Rule 10, Commentary 1)

Article 2.   BALL CROSSING THE NET—To be good, the ball must cross the net entirely between the antennas or their assumed indefinite extension.

Article 3.   PLAYER CONTACT WITH NET—If a player's action causes the player to contact the net during play, whether accidentally or not, with any part of the player's body or uniform, that player shall be charged with a fault. If the ball is driven into the net with such force that it causes the net to contact a player, such contact shall not be considered a fault.

Article 4.   SIMULTANEOUS CONTACT BY OPPONENTS—If opponents contact the net simultaneously, it shall constitute a double fault and the first referee shall direct a replay.

Article 5.   CONTACT BY PLAYER OUTSIDE THE NET—If a player accidentally contacts any part of the net supports (e.g. a post, cable), the referee's stand, etc., such contact should not be counted as a fault provided that it has no effect on the sequence of play. Intentional contact or grabbing of such objects shall be penalized as a fault.

Article 6.   CROSSING THE CENTER LINE—Contacting the opponent's playing area with any part of the body except the feet is a fault. Touching the opponent's area with a foot or feet is not a fault providing that some part of the encroaching foot or feet remain on or above the center line.
a)   It is not a fault to enter the opponent's side of the court after the ball has been declared dead by the first referee.
b)   It is not a fault to cross the assumed extension of the center line outside the playing area.
   (1)   While across the extension of the center line outside the court, a player of the attacking team may play a ball that has not fully passed beyond the plane of the net. Opponents may not interfere with a player making a play on the ball.
   (2)   A player who has crossed the extension of the center line and is not making a play on the ball may not interfere with an opponent.

Article 7.   BALL PENETRATING OR CROSS THE VERTICAL PLANE—A ball penetrating the vertical plane of the net over or below the net, whether over or outside the court, may be returned to the attacking team's side by a player of the attacking team provided the ball has not yet completely passed beyond the vertical plane of the net when such contact is made. A ball which has penetrated the vertical plane above the net may be played by either team.

COMMENTARY ON RULE 9
PLAY AT THE NET

1)   *BALL CROSSING VERTICAL PLANE OF THE NET*—*If a ball penetrates the vertical plane of the net over the net, under the net, or outside the antennas, the attacking team is allowed to attempt to play the ball back into their team area, providing the ball has not fully passed beyond the vertical plane of the net at the time of contact. The opponents are not allowed to intentionally touch the ball under the net before the ball passes fully beyond the vertical plane of the net. However, if the ball inadvertently contacts an opponent beyond the plane under the net, the ball becomes dead and is not considered to be a fault by the opponents.*
   a)   *Once the ball penetrates the vertical plane above the net, the opponents have equal right to play the ball.*

2)   *CONTACT WITH OPPONENT'S AREA*—*Contact with the opponent's area may only occur with a foot or feet. Contacting the opponent's area with a hand, or other part of the body other than a foot or feet, is a fault. If a player lands on an encroaching foot of an opponent, such contact is ignored unless, in the first referee's judgement, the act is done deliberately to interfere with an opponent.*

3)   *CONTACT WITH OPPONENT BEYOND THE VERTICAL PLANE*—*If a player makes contact with an opponent beyond the vertical plane of the net, and if such contact is inadvertent, the contact shall be ignored. If the contact is intentional, it shall be penalized by the referee without warning.*

a)   *Flagrant intentional contact shall result in disqualification of the player responsible for the contact.*

4)   *CROSSING THE CENTER LINE*—*It is not a fault to cross the center line onto the opponent's side of the net provided that no contact is made with the opponent's playing area. While across the center line extended, a member of the attacking team is permitted to make a play on the ball provided the ball has not passed fully beyond the vertical plane of the net at the time of contact.*

5)   *CONTACT WITH POSTS, CABLES, ETC*—*If a player accidently contacts a cable (including the cables supporting the net) or a post, cables supporting a post, referee stand, etc., it should not be counted as a fault unless it directly affects the subsequent sequence of play. If the stand, posts, etc., are intentionally grasped or used as a means of support, such action constitutes a fault.*

RULE 10.   LIVE BALL/DEAD BALL

Article 1.   WHEN BALL BECOMES ALIVE—The ball becomes alive when legally contacted for service.

Article 2.   WHEN BALL BECOMES DEAD—A live ball becomes dead when:

a)   The ball touches an antenna or the net outside an antenna.
b)   The ball does not cross the net completely between the antennas.
c)   The ball strikes the floor, floor obstructions or wall.
d)   The ball contacts the ceiling or overhead object at a height of 7 m. (23') or more above a playable surface, or any object above an unplayable area.
e)   A player(s) commits a fault.
f)   A served ball contacts the net or other object.
g)   The first or second referee blows a whistle, even though inadvertently.
h)   A player causes the ball to come to rest on a rafter or other overhead object that is less than 7 m. above the height of the playing surface.
i)   The ball contacts an object that is less than 15' above playable surface.

COMMENTARY ON RULE 10
DEAD BALL

1)   *INADVERTANT WHISTLE*—*The blowing of an inadvertent whistle causes the ball to become dead immediately. In such cases, the first referee must make a ruling that will not penalize either team. For instance, if the ball has been hit in such a manner that it is falling in an area where no player could logically make a play on the ball, and if the referee blows the whistle before the ball has touched the playing surface, by rule the ball becomes dead immediately. In this case, the first referee should rule as though the ball had touched the playing surface at the time the whistle blew. Another example would be after a third hit with the ball striking the net near the top and the first referee inadvertantly blowing the whistle. After the whistle, if the ball were to roll in such a manner that it crossed the net into the defending team's area, a replay should be called for by the first referee.*

2)   *WHISTLES AT APPROXIMATELY SAME TIME*—*If the second referee blows a whistle in response to a request by a captain or coach at approximately the same time as the first referee blows a whistle for service, play shall be stopped and the first referee shall determine which whistle was blown first. If the whistle of the second referee was blown before, or simultaneously with, the whistle for service, the request will be granted. If the whistle of the second referee was after the whistle for service, the request will be denied and a new service effort directed.*

3)   *BALL CONTACTING ANTENNA*—*If the ball contacts the antenna above or below the height of the net, the ball becomes dead.*

RULE 11.   TEAM AND PLAYER FAULTS

Article 1.   DOUBLE FAULT—A double fault occurs when players of opposing teams simultaneously commit faults. In such cases, the first referee will direct a play over.

Article 2.   FAULTS AT APPROXIMATELY THE SAME TIME—If faults by opponents occur at approximately the same time, the first referee shall determine which fault occurred first and shall penalize only that fault. If it cannot be determined which fault occurred first, a double fault shall be declared.

Article 3. PENALTY FOR COMMITTING FAULTS—If the serving team, or a player of the serving team, commits a fault, a side-out shall be declared. If the receiving team, or a player of the receiving team, commits a fault, the serving team shall be awarded a point.

Article 4. TEAM AND PLAYER FAULTS—A fault shall be declared against a team or player when:
a) The ball touches the floor (R. 10 A. 1)
b) The ball is held, thrown or pushed (R. 8 a. 6)
c) A team has played the ball more than three times consecutively (R. 8 A. 1) (EXCEPTION: R. 8 A. 11)
d) The ball touches a player below the waist (R. 8 A. 3)
e) A player touches the ball twice consecutively (R. 8 A. 5) (EXCEPTION: R. 8 A. 5 and A. 11)
f) A team is out of position at service (R. 7 A. 9)
g) A player touches the net or antenna (R. 9 A. 3)
h) A player completely crosses the center line and contacts the opponent's playing area (R. 8 A. 9)
i) A player attacks the ball above the opponent's playing area (R. 8 A. 9)
j) A back line player while in the attack area hits the ball into the opponent's court from above the height of the net (R. 8 A. 13)
k) A ball does not cross the net entirely between the antennas (R. 9 A. 2)
l) A ball lands outside the court or touches an object outside the court (R. 10 A. 1)
m) The ball is played by a player being assisted by a teammate as a means of support (R 8 A. 10)
n) A player reaches under the net and touches the ball or an opponent while the ball is being played by the opposite team (R. 9 C. 1)
o) Blocking is performed in an illegal manner (R. 8 A. 11)
p) Illegally served ball or service fault (R. 7 A. 2; R. 7 C. If)

RULE 12. SCORING AND RESULT OF THE GAME
Article 1. WHEN POINT IS SCORED—When a fault is committed by the receiving team, a point is awarded to the serving team.

Article 2. WINNING SCORE—A game is won when a team scores 15 points and has at least a two point advantage over the opponents. If the score is tied at 14-14, the play continues until one team has a lead of two points. (e.g. 16-14, 17-15, 18-16. etc.)

Article 3. SCORE OF DEFAULTED GAME—If a team does not have sufficient players to start a game, or fails to play after the first referee requests play to begin, that team shall lose the game by default. Score of each defaulted game will be 15-0.

Article 4. SCORE OF DEFAULTED GAME DUE TO INJURY—If a game is defaulted due to a team being reduced to less than six players because of an injury, the defaulting team shall retain any points earned. The winning team shall be credited with at least 15 points or will be awarded sufficient points to reflect a two point advantage over the opponents.

Article 5. SCORE OF DEFAULTED GAME DUE TO EXPULSION OF A PLAYER—If a game is defaulted due to expulsion or disqualification of a player, the defaulting team shall retain any points earned. The offended team shall be credited with at least 15 points or a sufficient number of points to indicate a two point winning advantage over the opponents.

Article 6. REFUSAL TO PLAY—If, after receiving a warning from the first referee, a team refuses to play, the entire match is defaulted. The score for each defaulted game is 15-0 and the score of the match is 2-0 or 3-0, depending upon the number of games scheduled for the match.

Article 7. INCOMPLETE TEAM DURING MATCH—If a team is reduced to less than six players and cannot complete the remainder of a match, the opponents shall be awarded sufficient points to reflect a winning score of 15 points, or more if 15 points do not provide a winning margin of at least 2 points, for the incomplete game and sufficient games necessary to win the match. The defaulting team keeps its points and games won.

COMMENTARY ON RULE 12
SCORING AND RESULTS OF THE GAME
1) *INSUFFICIENT PLAYERS TO START—If a team defaults a game due to failure to have sufficient players to start a game at the scheduled time, the score shall be recorded as 15-0. A waiting time of up to 15 minutes shall be allowed for the team to have sufficient players to play the next game. If the team has at least six players present prior to the expiration of the waiting time, play shall begin. If, after the 15 minute waiting period, a team does not have six players present and ready to play, the second game shall be declared a default. If the match consists of the best 3 out of 5 games, an additional 15 minute waiting period shall be allowed before declaring the match a default.*

a) *If neither team has six players available at match time, each team shall be charged with the loss of one game by default. The next game, if played, would be the third game of the match.*
b) *Score of each defaulted game is 15-0. Score of a defaulted match is 2-0 or 3-0, depending upon the number of games scheduled to be played.*

2) *FAILURE TO PLAY—If, during the progress of a game, a team fails to return to play for reasons other than a refusal to play, that team shall be charged a time-out. If it is the first or second team time-out, the team may use the time. If it results in a third time-out, the team shall be penalized (point or side out) and may not use the time. After an additional 15 seconds, if the team still has not returned to play, the game shall be declared a default. The losing team shall retain any points scored and the winning team shall be credited with sufficient points necessary to win the game. A two minute period shall then be granted for teams to change sides of the court and submit lineups for the next game of the match.*

3) *REFUSAL TO PLAY—After a signal from the first referee, teams shall immediately take their positions on the end line to start a match or game. At the conclusion of an interruption in play, teams shall return to their positions on the court immediately upon the signal of either referee. If a team refuses to do so, they shall be warned by the first referee. If, after the warning, the team still refuses to play, the game and match shall be defaulted. Score of each game will be 15-0 and the score of the match shall be 2-0 or 3-0, depending upon the number of games scheduled to be played.*

4) *DEFAULTED MATCH DURING PLAY—After play starts if a team is reduced to less than six players (due to injury, disqualification, etc.) and cannot complete the remainder of a match, the team loses the match by default. The defaulting team retains any games won and points scored during the game in which a default occurs.*

   The opponents are awarded sufficient points to reflect a winning score of 15 points, or additional points if 15 points will not result in a winning margin of at least two points, for the incompleted game. The winning team is also credited with sufficient games to win the match (2 games in a best of 3 match; 3 or 4 games in a best of 5 match).

5) *REPORTING FOR MATCH AND GAME—At the start of a match and at the expiration of the allowable rest period between games, teams must report immediately to the end line of their playing areas.*

a) *If a team fails to report to the end line of their playing area immediately upon the signal to begin a match or indicating the expiration of the period between games, that team shall be charged with a time-out. After 30 seconds, if the team has still failed to report to the end line, an additional time-out shall be charged. The team may use the 30 second time-out periods. If, after the expiration of the charged time-out, the team has not reported to the end line, the first referee shall penalize the offending team. If the team does not report immediately, a defaulted game shall be declared.*
b) *A two minute period shall begin immediately after a game has been declared defaulted by the first referee for failure of the team to report. During the two minute period, teams shall change sides and submit lineups for the next scheduled game.*
c) *If the same team again fails to report to the end line within the provisions of a) above, the match shall be declared a default by the first referee. A defaulted match shall be recorded as 2-0 or 3-0, depending upon the number of games scheduled.*

6) *DISCREPANCY IN SCORE—If there is a discrepancy between the scoring column and the running score column of the scoresheet, the running score column shall be the official score. If there is a discrepancy between the scoresheet and the visible scoring device, the scoresheet shall be the official score.*

RULE 13. DECISIONS AND PROTESTS
Article 1. AUTHORITY OF THE REFEREE—Decisions based on the judgement of the referee or other officials are final and not subject to protest.

Article 2. INTERPRETATION OF THE RULES—Disagreements with interpretations of the rules must be brought to the attention of the first referee prior to the first service following the play in which the disagreement occurred. The captain of the protesting team may be the only one to bring the protest to the attention of the first referee.

Article 3. APPEAL OF DECISION OF THE REFEREE—If the explanation of the first referee following a protest lodged by the team captain is not satisfactory, the captain may appeal to a higher authority. If the protest cannot be resolved, the first referee shall proceed to the scorer's table and shall record, or cause to be recorded, on the scoresheet all pertinent facts of the protest. After the facts of the protest have been recorded, the first referee will continue to direct the game and will forward a report later on the protest in question.

Article 4. DISAGREEMENT WITH THE REFEREE'S DECISION—If a team captain is in disagreement with a first referee's decision in the assessment of a sanction, such decision is not protestable, but the team captain may state such disagreement in writing on the back of the official scoresheet after completion of the match.

COMMENTARY ON RULE 13
DECISIONS AND PROTESTS

1) *PROTEST MATTERS NOT TO BE CONSIDERED—Protests involving the judgement of a referee or other officials will not be given consideration. Some of these items are:*
   a) *Whether or not a player on the court was out of position at service.*
   b) *Whether or not a ball was held or thrown.*
   c) *Whether or not a player's conduct should be penalized.*
   d) *Any other matters involving only the accuracy of an official's judgement.*

2) *PROTEST MATTERS TO BE CONSIDERED—Matters that shall be received and considered by the first referee concern:*
   a) *Misinterpretation of a playing rule.*
   b) *Failure of a first referee to apply the correct rule to a given situation.*
   c) *Failure to impose the correct penalty for a given violation.*

3) *RECORDING FACTS—The following facts should be recorded on the scoresheet concerning any protest situation:*
   a) *Score of the game at the time of the protest.*
   b) *Players in the game at the time of the protest and their positions on the court.*
   c) *Player substitutions and team substitutions made prior to the protested situation.*
   d) *Team time-outs charged prior to the protested situation.*
   e) *A synopsis of the situation that caused the protest and the rule violated or omitted or the penalty improperly imposed.*
   f) *Signatures of the scorer, both team captains and the first referee, to indicate that the facts have been correctly recorded.*

4) *PROTEST COMMITTEE ACTION—Where possible in tournament play, it is advisable to have a protest committee assigned and available to rule upon a protest situation as soon as possible, preferably prior to the first service following the protest. Such action will preclude having to play the match over from the point of protest if the protest is upheld. The situation can be immediately corrected and only the play in question played over.*
   a) *During sanctioned USVBA competition, the protest committee will rule upon the protested game immediately upon its completion and before another game of the match is played.*

5) *PROTEST RULING AND EFFECT—After considering the facts of the protest, the ruling authority may rule that the protest was valid and should be upheld or that the protest is not valid and should be denied. If the protest is upheld, the game will be replayed from the moment in the game immediately preceding the play which prompted the lodging of a protest. If the protest is denied, the score and situation will remain as though the protest had never been lodged.*
   a) *If the protested game creates the necessity for additional games to be played, only the additional games necessary to determine a winner of the match shall be played.*

6) *DISAGREEMENT WITH REFEREE'S DECISION—If a team captain feels that the assessing of a sanction by the first referee is unwarranted or too severe, such disagreement may be expressed on the scoresheet by the team captain after the conclusion of the match. The first referee will not permit complaints about decisions pertaining to ball handling, or other similar judgement situations pertaining to the playing of the ball, to be recorded on the scoresheet.*

CHAPTER IV
OFFICIALS AND THEIR DUTIES

NOTE: Chapter IV is included as a guideline for officials and shall not be construed to be a part of the official playing rules subject to protest by teams.

RULE 14. THE FIRST REFEREE
Article 1. AUTHORITY OF THE FIRST REFEREE—The first referee is in full control of the match and any judgement decisions rendered by the first referee are final. The first referee has authority over all players and officials from the coin toss prior to the first game of a match until the conclusion of the match, to include any periods during which the match may be temporarily interrupted, for whatever reason.

Article 2. QUESTIONS NOT COVERED BY RULE—The first referee has the power to settle all questions, including those not specifically covered in the rules.

Article 3. POWER TO OVERRULE—The first referee has the power to overrule decisions of other officials when, in the first referee's opinion, they have made errors.

Article 4. POSITION OF FIRST REFEREE DURING MATCH—The first referee shall be located at one end of the net in a position that will allow a clear view of the play. The referee's head should be approximately 50 cm. (19 1/2") above the top of the net.

Article 5. PENALIZING VIOLATIONS—In accordance with Rule 4 the first referee penalizes violations made by players, coaches and other team members.

Article 6. USE OF SIGNALS—Immediately after giving a signal to stop play, the first referee shall indicate with the use of hand signals the nature of the violation, if a player fault, the player committing the fault and the team which shall make the next service.

COMMENTARY ON RULE 14
THE FIRST REFEREE

1) *SIGNALING SERVICE—The first referee will blow a whistle at the beginning of each play to indicate that service shall begin and at any other time judged to be necessary.*

2) *INTERRUPTING PLAY—Each action is considered finished when the first referee blows a whistle, other than that to indicate service. Generally speaking, the first referee should only interrupt the play when certain that a fault has been committed, and should not blow the whistle if there is any doubt.*

3) *TIME-OUTS—After a time-out, signals the number of time-outs that have been taken by each team.*

4) *REQUESTING ASSISTANCE—Should the first referee need to deal with anything outside the limits of the court, the first referee should request help from the organizer and players.*

5) *OVERRULING OFFICIALS—If the referee is certain that one of the other officials has made an incorrect decision, the first referee has the power to overrule that official and apply the correct decision. If the first referee feels that one of the other officials is not correctly fulfilling duties outlined by the Rules, the referee may have the official replaced.*

6) *SUSPENDING THE MATCH—Should an interruption occur, particularly if spectators should invade the court, the referee must suspend the match and ask organizers and the captain of the home team to re-establish order within a set period of time. If the interruption continues beyond this period of time, or if one of the teams refuses to continue playing, the first referee must instruct other officials to leave the court along with the first referee. The first referee must record the incident on the scoresheet and forward a report to the proper authority within 24 hours.*

7) *AUTHORITY OF THE REFEREE—Although the referee is in full control of the match and any judgement decisions rendered are considered final, this in no way relieves the right of team captains to protest and record matters allowed under provisions of Rule 13, Article 3.*

RULE 15. THE SECOND REFEREE

Article 1. POSITION DURING MATCH—The second referee shall take a position on the side of the court opposite and facing the first referee.

Article 2. ASSISTING THE FIRST REFEREE—The second referee shall assist the first referee by making calls such as:

a) Violations of the center line and attack line.
b) Contact with the net by a player.
c) Contact of the ball with an antenna or not crossing the net entirely inside the antenna on the second referee's side of the court.
d) Foreign objects entering the court and presenting a hazard to the safety of players.
e) Calling back court attacker/blocker violations.
f) Performing duties in addition to those outlined when instructed to do so by the first referee.

Article 3. KEEPING OFFICIAL TIME—The second referee shall be responsible for keeping official time of time-outs and rest periods between games of match.

Article 4. CONDUCT OF PARTICIPANTS—The second referee shall supervise the conduct of coaches and substitutes on the bench and shall call to the attention of first referee any unsportsmanlike actions of players or other team members.

Article 5. SUPERVISION OF SUBSTITUTIONS—The second referee shall authorize substitutions requested by captains or the head coach of the teams.

Article 6. SERVICE ORDER OF TEAMS—The second referee shall verify at the beginning of each game that players of both teams are on the court in positions corresponding with lineups submitted to the scorer. The second referee shall supervise the rotation order and positions of the receiving team at the time of service.

Article 7. GIVING OPINIONS—The second referee shall give opinions on all matters when so requested by the first referee.

Article 8. ENDING PLAY—The play is considered as ended when the second referee blows a whistle.

COMMENTARY ON RULE 15
THE SECOND REFEREE

1) *KEEPING OFFICIAL TIME—It is the responsibility of the second referee to keep the official time during time-outs, and between games of a match. When a time-out is charged, the second referee will signal the first refereee the number of time-outs that have been charged to each team. At the expiration of the time-out, the second referee shall signal the number of time-outs each team has taken.*

2) *SUBSTITUTIONS—The second referee will authorize a substitution when the substitute is ready to enter the game. Before allowing the substitute to enter the court, the second referee will make certain that the scorer has the necessary information to properly record the substitution.*

3) *CONTROL OF THE BALL—The second referee shall be responsible for the ball during interruptions of play.*

4) *REPLACING FIRST REFEREE—Should the first referee suddenly be indisposed, is shall be the responsibility of the second referee to assume the duties of first referee.*

5) *ASSISTING REFEREE—The second referee will make calls and perform duties in addition to those outlined when instructed to do so by the first referee.*

6) *VERIFYING LINEUPS—When teams change courts during the middle of a deciding game of a match, it is the duty of the second referee to verify that players of both teams are in their correct service order as listed on the scoresheet.*

7) *GIVING INFORMATION TO TEAM CAPTAINS—Upon request of a team captain for verification that the opponents are in their correct service order or that players are not in the game illegally, the first referee may direct the second referee to verify that the players are correct or incorrect. No direct identification of opposing players will be given to the team captain. Requests for such information by team captains will be limited to infrequent occasions. If it is found that the players are in an incorrect position or illegally in the game, the first referee will direct the second referee and scorer to correct the error.*

RULE 16. THE SCORER

Article 1. POSITION DURING MATCH—The scorer's position is on the side of the court opposite the first referee and behind the second referee.

Article 2. RECORDING INFORMATION—Prior to the start of a match, the scorer will clearly print the names of the 1st referee, 2nd referee and scorer on the scoresheet. The scorer will obtain the lineup sheets and record the numbers of the starting players on the scoresheet. Once a lineup or team roster has been submitted to the scorer, no changes may be made. Between games of the match, the scorer reminds the second referee to obtain new lineups from the captains or coaches in order to properly record any changes in the lineups. In addition, the scorer:

a) Verifies the team rosters prior to the start of the match.
b) records the scores as the match progresses.
c) makes sure that the serving order and rotation of players is followed correctly.
d) carefully checks the eligibility of substitutes before authorizing their entry into a game.
e) Records substitution information on the scoresheet.
f) records time-outs and notifies the second referee and the first referee of the number of time-outs which have been charged to each team.

Article 3. DURING DECIDING GAME OF MATCH—During the deciding game of a match the scorer signals the referees when one of the team has scored an eighth point and indicates that the teams should change playing areas.

Article 4. VERIFICATION OF FINAL SCORE—At the conclusion of a game, the scorer verifies the final results of the game by signing the appropriate block of the scoresheet.

COMMENTARY ON RULE 16
THE SCORER

1) *GIVING INFORMATION TO TEAMS—The scorer, when requested to do so by one of the referees, must tell either of the coaches or captains the number of substitutions and time-outs that have been charged to their team. Information pertaining to opponents will not be given to a coach or captain by the scorer.*

2) *LINEUPS—Prior to the start of each game of a match, the coach or team captain must send a lineup to the scorer on the official form provided. Prior to the start of play, opponents will not be permitted to see the lineup submitted by the opposing team.*

3) *RECORDING OF REMARKS—The scorer must record all remarks pertaining to penalties, protests, etc., that occur during the progress of the game.*

4) *ORDER OF SERVICE—The scorer must control the order of service. If a wrong server is in the service position at the time the referee whistles for service, the scorer shall wait until the ball is contacted during service and then sound a horn/whistle and notify the referees of the fault.*

5) *THE SCORE—The scorer must record each point made by a team. The scorer must make sure that the score on the visible scoreboard agrees with the score recorded on the scoresheet. In the event of a discrepancy, the scoresheet shall be official and the discrepancy is not grounds for protest by a team.*

6) *Results of games are final and official when the scoresheet is signed by the scorer.*

RULE 17. THE LINE JUDGES

Article 1. POSITION DURING MATCH—During the match, the line judges will be stationed:

a) With two line judges, they must be placed diagonally opposite each other, one at each end of the court at the corner away from the service area near the intersection of the end line and side boundary line.
b) With four line judges, one line judge shall be placed opposite each service area with the sideline extended approximately 2 m. behind the end line. One line judge shall be placed approximately 2 m. outside the sideline nearest the service area

in line with the end line extended. Each line judge watches the line to which assigned.

Article 2.   DUTIES—Line judges shall signal the first referee when:
a) Ball lands inbounds (Signal 3 or Signal 2)
b) Ball lands out of bounds (Signal 5 or Signal 4)
c) Foot fault by server or other player (Signal 8 or Signal 2)
d) Ball touches, passes over or outside an antenna (Signal 8 or Signal 4)
e) Ball contacts player before going out of bounds (Signal 7 or Signal 6)
f) Ball contacts overhead object (Signal 25)

Article 3.   SIGNAL FLAGS—The use of signal flags by line judges shall be at the discretion of the first referee.

COMMENTARY ON RULE 17
THE LINE JUDGES

1) POSITION DURING MATCH—During the match, line judges shall be standing in their assigned areas and shall move from those areas only for the purpose of avoiding interfering with players playing the ball or to better observe a ball crossing the net near an antenna.

2) NUMBER OF LINE JUDGES—For important competitions, it is recommended that four line judges be used.

3) SIGNALING THE FIRST REFEREE—Whenever a line judge needs to attract the attention of the first referee due to a fault committed by a player, or to a rude remark made by a player, the flag or hands shall be raised above the head and waved from side to side.

GAME PROCEDURES

These are the recommended standard procedures to be followed for the conduct of all official USVBA competition:

1. **OFFICIALS**
   a) The officials should be certified referees and scorers of the United States Volleyball Association.

2. **UNIFORMS**
   a) All players must wear uniforms prescribed by USVBA rule 5.
   b) All non-playing referees must wear the official uniform described in Section 4 of the USVBA Guide.

3. **PRE-GAME PROCEDURES**
   a) Well ahead of starting time for the first game of a match, the first referee will call team captains together and conduct a coin toss.
   b) After the coin toss, the first referee will supervise warm-up periods with the serving team having use of the court for the first three minute warm-up period if the captains have elected to use separate warm-ups. If the team captains elect to warm-up together on the court, the first referee shall allow six minutes.
   c) At the end of the warm-up period, the first or second referee will walk to the center of the court and blow a whistle to indicate that the warm-up period is over and players are to clear the court.
   d) Referees and other officials take their places.
   e) Teams line up on the end line of their respective areas. When both teams are ready and facing each other, the first referee will blow a whistle and motion for teams to take their positions on the court.
   f) Second referee will verify that players are on the court in positions listed on the official lineup sheets submitted to the scorer by each team. No corrections may be made unless there has been an error or omission made by the scorer or unless a legal substitution has been made prior to the start of play under the provisions of rule 5, Commentary 7 b. No other changes may be made in the lineups to correct an error made by teams in preparing the lineup sheets.

4. **START OF THE GAME**
   a) As soon as lineups are verified and teams are ready, the whistle is blown and a visual sign is given by the first referee for service to begin.
   b) Prior to the serve, offensive players will halt their movements to allow officials to determine their positions. Continual movement may be misconstrued as screening.

5. **SUBSTITUTION PROCEDURES**
   a) Substitutes should approach the second referee in the substitution zone and wait to be recognized for entry. Substitutes entering the court and players leaving the court shall touch hands in the substitution zone and wait to be authorized to enter by the second referee.

6. **END OF GAME AND START OF NEXT GAME**
   a) Following the blowing of a whistle indicating the end of a game, players should line up on the end line of their playing areas. When both teams are in position and the second referee has verified that the winning point has been recorded, the first referee will blow a whistle and dismiss the teams for the rest period between games. Players may then leave the court.
   b) At the end of the rest period, the second referee will blow a whistle and teams shall immediately report to the end of their playing areas for the next game.

7. **CHANGE OF PLAYING AREAS DURING GAME**
   a) When teams are required to change playing areas during a deciding game of a match, the first referee will blow a whistle and indicate both teams to move to the end line of their respective playing areas.
   b) After both teams are in position, the first referee will blow a whistle and motion for both teams to proceed in a counter-clockwise direction to the opposite end without delay.
   c) Substitutes and other team personnel will change benches so as to be seated adjacent to their playing area.
   d) When teams are in position on the end line of the new playing areas, the first referee will blow a whistle and motion for both teams to move onto the court.
   e) The second referee will then verify that players are in their correct positions on the court.

8. **AT THE END OF THE MATCH**
   a) Following the whistle indicating the end of a match, players will line up on the end line of their respective playing areas.
   b) When both teams are in position and the second referee has verified that the winning point has been recorded by the scorer, the first referee will blow a whistle and motion for teams to form a single line and proceed to the center of the court to shake hands with opponents.
   c) The second referee will assure that the game ball is returned to the designated area for safekeeping.
   d) Referees will then immediately depart the area of the court.

COMMENTARY ON GAME PROCEDURES

1) SUBSTITUTES ENTERING GAME—Substitutes entering the game shall wait in the substitution zone until authorized to enter by the second referee. If a player enters without authorization, the player shall be directed to return to the substitution zone and the team warned by the first referee. While there is no intent to make protocol a major part of the game, failure of a player(s) to follow proper procedures can cause errors in the recording of information by scorers.

2) VERIFICATION OF SCORESHEETS—At the conclusion of each game, the second referee will check with the scorer to assure that a winning score has been attained and will then notify the first referee. The scorer will then verify the final official score of the game by signing the scoresheet in the appropriate block on the scoresheet.

THE USVBA: DEVELOPING PROGRAMS TO SERVE THE VOLLEYBALL COMMUNITY

The United States Volleyball Association (USVBA) is the country's national governing body for the sport. The USVBA's aim is to foster the growth of the game so that all Americans can have the opportunity to participate. The USVBA is affiliated with the United States Olympic Committee and is the exclusive representative of the nation to the Fédération Internationale de Volleyball and to a number of other international bodies.

The USVBA's involvements vary from the highest level of international competition, through the USA Men's and Women's Teams to grassroots competition, through USVBA regions and member organizations to the development of quality coaching and participation through such programs as USA Coaching Accreditation, U.S. Junior Olympic Volleyball, and USA Youth Volleyball.

Beginning in the late seventies and leading up to 1984, a major focus of the USVBA was the success of the USA Men's and Women's Teams in international competition. By establishing a year-round training program for the teams and through extensive competition against the world's best, the USA has established a tradition of excellence for its national teams. Olympic gold and silver medal victories for the USA Men's and Women's Teams in 1984 served as a milestone in the sport's rise to recognition, not only internationally, but also in the eyes of the American public. The USA Teams have continued to perform well internationally, and the USA Men won the '85 World Cup, '86 World Championships, and the 1988 Olympic gold medal.

After 1984, the USVBA not only continued to train its USA Men's and Women's Teams for world-class performance, but also moved into focus an effort to expand opportunities for participation to children and teens in this country. The USA Youth Volleyball program was established in earnest, and today programs for boys and girls, ages 7 to 12, are springing up throughout the United States. Boys' and Girls' Clubs of America, YMCAs, park and recreation departments, and other recreation agencies are offering coaching instructional clinics and initiating USA Youth Volleyball programs for children.

At the teen level, the U.S. Junior Olympic Volleyball program offers competition for boys and girls ages 18 and under, 16 and under, and 14 and under. Participation in Junior Olympic Volleyball is administered through the USVBA regions and is an off-season complement to many interscholastic programs. Competition for this age group culminates in the U.S. Junior Olympic Volleyball Championships.

Adults also participate in competition administered by USVBA regions. The U.S.

Open Volleyball Championship is the national championship for men and women, with tournaments in age divisions ranging from open competition to the golden masters division. A national coed tournament, the U.S. Coed Volleyball Championships, is also conducted annually by the USVBA.

The USVBA is not merely concerned with athletic excellence, but also conducts programs for the development of quality coaching and officiating. In addition to the Volleyball Colloquium and Volleyball Symposium clinics, USA Youth Volleyball instructor clinics, IMPACT clinics, and those for volleyball referees and scorekeepers, the USVBA has established the USA Coaching Accreditation Program (CAP). Incorporating the American Coaching Effectiveness Program (ACEP), CAP is a comprehensive, four-level coaching education program, with clinics offered throughout the United States. CAP is intended to offer a foundation for advancement in the volleyball coaching profession.

To learn more about the USVBA and its programs, contact the national office, 1750 East Boulder Street, Colorado Springs, CO 80909, telephone 719-578-4750.